THE
SOUTHERN
AFTER STEAM

A Vision in Blue and Grey

Cover Shots

On 26 January 1982 Slim Jim 33.209 stands at Paddock Wood with the 1003 Dover Docks to Paddock Wood Tranfesa vans from Spain.

23 May 1984. Unit 1036 on the rear of the 0840 Hastings to Charing Cross at High Brooms. 1035 is the front unit.

On 10 March 1983 MLV 68007 leads a 12 CEP formation on the 1332 Dover Marine (1005 from Oostende) to Victoria at Biddenden Green, near Pluckley.

THE SOUTHERN AFTER STEAM

A Vision in Blue and Grey

DON BENN

PEN & SWORD
TRANSPORT

AN IMPRINT OF PEN & SWORD BOOKS LTD.
YORKSHIRE – PHILADELPHIA

First published in Great Britain in 2019 by
Pen and Sword Transport
An imprint of
Pen & Sword Books Ltd
Yorkshire - Philadelphia

ISBN 978 1 52670 008 7

Typeset in Times New Roman by Aura Technology and Software Services, India.

Printed and bound in India by Replika Press Pvt. Ltd.

Pen & Sword Books Ltd incorporates the Imprints of Pen & Sword Books Archaeology, Atlas, Aviation, Battleground, Discovery, Family History, History, Maritime, Military, Naval, Politics, Railways, Select, Transport, True Crime, Fiction, Frontline Books, Leo Cooper, Praetorian Press, Seaforth Publishing, Wharncliffe and White Owl.

For a complete list of Pen & Sword titles please contact

PEN & SWORD BOOKS LIMITED
47 Church Street, Barnsley, South Yorkshire, S70 2AS, England
E-mail: enquiries@pen-and-sword.co.uk
Website: www.pen-and-sword.co.uk

Or
PEN AND SWORD BOOKS
1950 Lawrence Rd, Havertown, PA 19083, USA
E-mail: Uspen-and-sword@casematepublishers.com
Website: www.penandswordbooks.com

CONTENTS

PREFACE

Although I am better known for my books and articles on steam, I was brought up and have lived all my life in Southern Electric territory, being born in Sydenham and then living in St Mary Cray, Bromley, West Wickham, Ashford (Kent), Paddock Wood, Robertsbridge and now Locks Heath near to Swanwick on the Fareham to Southampton line. It is therefore natural that I have always had a keen interest in Southern electric and diesel stock, though the modern scene doesn't attract me as much as the traditional stock. My library of negatives from the early years of my pursuit of photography contains many shots of Southern EMUs as well as steam. Many hours were spent on the footbridge at Bromley South station or at Bickley or Orpington. Also from very early days I made use of day rover tickets to

Bromley South on Sunday, 12 February 1961. 4 EPB 5216 is reversing into the up platform having terminated with a Victoria to Orpington stopping service. In the background can be seen the footbridge where the author spent so many happy hours and witnessed the end of steam working in the area. Note that the headcode blinds haven't been changed.

BR design 1960 built 4 EPB 5338 at Bromley South on an up train when new in August 1960.

Bickley, September 1960. CEP 7128 on a Victoria to Ramsgate service. In the carriage siding is a 4 EPB unit in the 1957 Phase 1 series.

4 EPB 5344 shunts back through the carriage washer and into the shed at Orpington, September 1960

Guildford, 18 September 1960. 2 BIL unit 2067 on a stopping service from Waterloo to Portsmouth and Southsea. Although 2 BILs were built in batches for specific schemes they were over time moved around. However, in this picture 2067 is on 'home ground' and on a working it was originally intended for, having been built as part of the batch for the Portsmouth No. 2 electrification scheme.

explore the Southern empire further afield and was fascinated by the pre-war stock still running in the early 1960s on the Central and South Western Divisions. Very few shots were taken in colour as this was reserved for special occasions, such as the last day of the Westerham branch on 28 October 1961 when I took the shot at Elmers End on the way to Dunton Green. After the end of steam on the Southern in July 1967, I concentrated primarily on recording the Southern scene, to start with in black and white and then from 1972 in colour using mainly 35mm Kodachrome 25 film with a Praktica, and later from 1977 'until it was stolen' my trusty Pentax KX with a variety of lenses. I also used a Bronica 6x4.5 camera with Ektachrome slide film from about 1981 for a few years. In so doing I built up a huge collection of slides for the period 1972 to 1988. After that my time for the next ten years was spent trying to run a transport business and I didn't really resume my railway interests until the digital era which began for me in 2005. All this therefore explains the period which this book covers. I tended to concentrate on the lines close to home or in the London area and so there is some bias in that respect, for which I make no apology. In fact there is very little of EMUs on the Central and South Western Division main lines. I also tried to record as many loco-hauled trains as possible and there was a surprising amount of that in the period covered plus of course chasing the unusual. Recording on film and with my stopwatch the final years of classes was

Elmers End, 28 October 1961. 2 EPB unit 5706 has just arrived from Addiscombe. This platform is now used by the Croydon Tramlink.

London Bridge, August 1971. The evening rush hour on the South Eastern side. A selection of EPB units including 5034 leading a Hayes to Charing Cross service, headcode 34.

also paramount and if I had to choose my all-time favourite Southern unit class then it would have to be the Hastings DEMUs. This book is primarily a colour photo album but I have included some details of the trains in the introduction to each section and also representative train performance logs, many from the 1960s. As I didn't start colour slide photography until late August 1972, I only have black-and-white shots of the last of the pre-war stock, the 4 COR units, in normal service, and of the *Brighton Belle* and the

Golden Arrow, all of which finished during 1972, so these are included for completeness. As far as the multiple units are concerned this book only covers the second generation stock and not therefore the replacements such as the 455s and 508s which were gradually introduced from the late 1970s. I scanned over 1,000 slides out of a total of about 10,000 for this book and so choosing the final selection meant that about three quarters of the scans have been set aside, maybe for another book?

INTRODUCTION

Each section contains some details of the main classes of units and locomotives featured in this book as they were at the end of 1979. This isn't intended to be complete or to cover all the variations or revised formations within each class but is to set the scene for the photographs which follow. Most of the multiple units and the Southern Region based locomotives were renumbered from the early 1980s. I haven't included full details of remaining pre-war stock which just lasted into 1972, though there are a few images of them, including some of the preserved stock. In 1972 sectorisation was still in the future and all over blue was common with suburban stock. From 1980 blue and grey became the norm for suburban stock, though main-line stock had used this livery since the late 1960s. Inter City and Freight sector liveries also came onto the scene. I have used the traditional Southern Region number classification throughout for multiple units, e.g. CEP not 411. The superb Network South East was established in 1986, bringing its vivid 'toothpaste' colour scheme, unifying not only the former Southern Region but all of London and the South-East, and somewhat beyond. In addition to the indigenous stock, I have included the Western Region units which worked right across Southern territory through Guildford and Redhill to Tonbridge and the class 47s which appeared on Inter Regional trains and on some freight on the South Western Division.

CHAPTER ONE
PRE-WAR ELECTRIC MULTIPLE UNIT STOCK

1936 Stock: The 4 SUB Class 405

By 1972 none of the pre-war SUB stock was left, and remaining units were numbered in the 4277-4299 and 4617-4754 series which were introduced from October 1948 to 1952. Most of the 4 SUB class were fitted with EE339 traction motors rated at 275 hp with suburban gearing, though this didn't stop determined drivers reaching some extraordinary high speeds down Brockley bank, as shown in the train running logs. `Table 1` – *See Page 27*. Sixty mph London area speed limit? It was totally ignored by most drivers. The 1952 batch of 4 SUB was fitted with the lighter weight EE507 traction motors. In the period covered by the book the 4 SUBs worked suburban trains on the Central and South Western Divisions. There was progressive withdrawal of earlier builds from 1972, and following service reductions forty-nine units were withdrawn in 1976 and all were gone by the end of 1983, though unit 4732 is preserved and was used on the main line for a while. They never carried the blue and grey livery so they are all in overall blue in this book.

Waterloo on 21 April 1983. Passengers are boarding 4 SUBs 4668 and 4291 on the 1612 to Effingham Junction. In the background are the first floor offices where I worked in the days of steam in 1966.

On 7 July 1977, 4 SUB No. 4617 is leaving Clapham Junction with the 1156 Shepperton to Waterloo. The down fast platform from where this shot was taken is surprisingly quiet.

Turning round I caught 4 SUB No. 4617 on the 1156 Shepperton to Waterloo meeting No. 4657 on the 1234 Waterloo to Shepperton. In the background is Signal Box A minus its cladding. This is the signal box which collapsed on 10 May 1965 causing considerable disruption to services. Today of course all lines would have been closed for days if not weeks while blame was apportioned. Interesting adulterated rear headcode illumination window on 4617, and the unit number is a clean patch.

Another shot at the same location. 4 SUBs 4279 and 4629 arrive at Clapham Junction on a Kingston Roundabout service on 24 November 1982.

On 18 February 1983, 4 SUBs 4719 and 4278 enter Clapham cutting on the down slow line with the 1404 Waterloo to Shepperton. On the right are the Brighton lines and on the left, listed right to left, are the South Western up slow down and up fast lines.

Earlier the same day, 18 February 1983, 4 SUBs 4719 and 4278 leave Wimbledon on the down slow line, past a remarkably empty yard, with the 1204 Waterloo to Shepperton. On the left is the footpath where I spent many hours taking photographs in the days of steam.

Further out from London, 4 SUBs 4620 leading 4657 leave Bookham on the 1012 Waterloo to Effingham Junction on 27 October 1982.

The same 4 SUBs '4657 trailing 4620 near Bookham' returning with the 1114 Effingham Junction to Waterloo on 27 October 1982.

At the same location near Bookham, 4 SUBs 4743 and 4751 head the 1038 Victoria to Effingham Junction, 27 October 1982.

26 July 1983. 4 SUBs 4629 and 4278 at Clapham Junction with the 1423 Beckenham Junction to Victoria. The classic view of the up slow Brighton line at this location.

Clapham Junction, 18 February 1983. 4 SUBs 4747 and 4742 on a Victoria to Effingham Junction via Mitcham Junction service. Hardly suburban!

Clapham Junction again but this time on 25 January 1980. Looking resplendent in the winter sun, 4 SUB 4643 arrives at Clapham Junction with the 1113 Victoria to Beckenham Junction. An 08 diesel shunter lurks over in the South Western Division yard no doubt waiting for some empty stock to shunt.

Leaving Clapham Junction on 21 April 1983, 4 SUBs 4743 and 4726 are working the 1519 Victoria to East Croydon.

It's now summer at the same location as the previous shot and 4 SUBs 4278 and 4277 are working the 1505 Victoria to Epsom Downs on 26 July 1983. Taken with a different telephoto lens to the previous shot.

A couple of shots at Wandsworth Common on 25 January 1980. First 4 SUB 4295 on the 1134 Victoria to Effingham Junction via Mitcham Junction.

Now at Wandsworth Common station on the same fine winter's day, 4 SUB 4290 on the 1143 Victoria to Beckenham Junction. This was another favourite location for down trains though not so good for those going to Victoria.

At the same location on a warm 30 September 1982, sister 4 SUB to the one in the previous shot, 4291, is on the 1413 Victoria to Beckenham Junction. I would often wait to see what the weather forecast was before taking a day off work to travel to London to capture trains working in the sun.

There were many fine days in the Autumn of 1982, and here at Norbury 4 SUB 4674 is on an empty stock working from Selhurst Depot to Victoria, again on 30 September 1982. As it's 1540 in the afternoon this unit is likely to be running up to join another 4 SUB unit for the evening peak. We had moved from Wandsworth Common in 4 SUB 4726.

From Norbury on 30 September 1982, we moved to Crystal Palace in 4 SUB 4750 to Balham and 4291 from there. Here SUB units were working the West Croydon and Beckenham Junction services. 4730 is on the 1614 Victoria to Beckenham Junction.

Other Pre-War Stock

This includes the 4 CORs, 2 BILs and *Brighton Belle* (5 BEL) Units. The *Belle* finished at the end of April 1972 and the CORs, originally built for the Portsmouth Direct and Mid-Sussex Lines electrifications, lingered on working Coastway services until 30 September 1972. One 4 COR driving car is preserved as part of the National Collection but a complete unit and an additional driving car are preserved by the Southern

Electric Group. Parts of the SEG's unit are (at the time of writing) in regular service as locomotive-hauled coaches on the East Kent Railway. The final day of regular public service for the 2 BILs was 29 July 1971 but one unit is preserved as part of the National Collection and photos are included. The Brighton Belle Trust is currently restoring 5 BEL vehicles for main-line running. Other *Brighton Belle* vehicles are still in existence and some are in service as locomotive-hauled coaches.

5 BEL units 3051 and 3052 approaching Clapham Junction on the last 1100 Victoria *Brighton Belle* on 29 April 1972.

On the last day of 4 COR working on East Coastway services, 30 September 1972, Unit 3123 leaves Hastings with the 0811 Ore to Eastbourne.

9 December 1972. 4 COR 3142 stands at Bognor Regis with the 1015 *Nelson Farewell* from Brighton. The train reversed here and ran to Victoria via the Arun Valley line, Dorking and Mitcham Junction, arriving in London three minutes early at 1312. The other units were 3123 and 3116.

Still at Bognor Regis on 9 December 1972, 4 COR Units 3116 and 3123 wait with the 1015 *Nelson Farewell* from Brighton as 2 SAP unit 5630 arrives with a Coastway service. From Victoria the train ran round to Waterloo and then to Portsmouth Harbour via the direct line. The first part of this fine run is shown. After Guildford a maximum speed of 83 mph was recorded at Liss. Table 2 – *See Page 28.*

2 BIL 2090 and 4 SUB 4732 climb to Somerhill tunnel on the Hastings Line outside Tonbridge with the 0715 special from Brighton on 10 May 1986.

24 August 1986 at London Bridge. 2 BIL 2090 and 4 SUB 4732 on the 1325 special working from Cannon Street. The special workings were shuttle services for the Network SouthEast arranged Greenwich 150 event at Cannon Street.

Tables

Table 1

4 SUBs . EAST CROYDON TO NEW CROSS GATE

		1817 East Croydon to London Bridge				1817 East Croydon to London Bridge			
Train		1817 East Croydon to London Bridge				1817 East Croydon to London Bridge			
Date		10 October 1968				10 April 1969			
Units		4736 + 4 SUB				4122+4720			
Timed by		Author				Author			

	miles	Sched	mins	secs	speed	Sched	mins	secs	speed
Norwood Junction	0.00	0.00	00	00		0.00	00	00	
MP 8¼	0.44		01	04	40½		00	57	40
Anerley	1.10		01	53	51		01	46	51
Penge West	1.50		02	23	54½		02	15	55½
Sydenham	2.19		03	03	60		02	58	60
Forest Hill	3.06		03	54	64		03	48	62
MP 5½	3.19		04	02	64½		03	55	64½
Honor Oak Park	3.95		04	39	70½		04	34	70
MP 4	4.69		05	16	75		05	11	77½
Brockley	4.99		05	27	78		05	22	80
MP 3½	5.19		05	40	76		05	34	76
New Cross Gate	5.81	9.00	06	30		9.00	06	18	

Table 2

4 CORs- WATERLOO TO WOKING

Date	9 December 1972
Train	The *Nelson Farewell* 1408 Waterloo to Portsmouth Harbour
Units	4 CORS 3116, 3123 and 3142
Load	12 coaches
Crew	Driver Musgrove and Inspector Reynolds
Weather	Fine
Recorder	Author

	miles	sched	mins	secs	speed
Waterloo	0.00	0.00	00	00	
Vauxhall	1.29		02	30	45
Queens Road	2.81		04	05	60
Clapham Junction	3.93	6.30	05	33	37*
Earlsfield	5.58		07	36	57
Wimbledon	7.24		09	18	61
Raynes Park	8.64		10	37	64½
New Malden	9.78		11	39	66½
Berrylands	10.98		12	44	67
Surbiton	12.04		13	39	70
Hampton Court Jct	13.34	17.00	14	44	72½
Esher	14.39		15	36	74
Hersham	15.91		16	52	75
Walton	17.08		17	49	73
Oatlands Box	18.10		18	40	70½
Weybridge	19.15		19	29	74
Byfleet and New Haw	20.40		20	33	76
West Byfleet	21.68		21	34	74
Woking	24.29	27.00	24	08	30*
	times and speeds to pass Woking				

CHAPTER TWO

1951 AND 1957 ELECTRIC MULTIPLE UNIT STOCK

4 EPB
1951 SR design stock (Class 415/1)
5001-5053, 5101-5264, 5401-5404 1957 BR
design stock (Class 415/2) 5301-5370

2 EPB
1951 SR design stock (Class 416/1) 5651-5684
(6301-6334) 1957 BR design stock (Class 416/2)
5702-5779 (6202-6279), 5781-5795

EPB (Electro Pneumatic Brake) Suburban units were introduced from 1951 to Southern Railway design and to BR design. They had EE507 traction motors rated at 250hp, again with suburban gearing, giving 1,000 hp per four-coach unit. Their use was widespread on all three divisions, though mainly in the London Suburban area. Units 5781-5795 were built in 1954/55 for use on the Newcastle and South Shields line and transferred to the Southern in 1963 after the line was de-electrified. They could easily be identified by the

larger guard's van section and shallower headcode blind windows. Once again the EPBs could be very speedy in the right hands as these two logs, again down Brockley bank, show, Table 3 – *See Page 73*, though the next log shows the sort of normal work that they did. Table 4 – *See Page 74*. All EPBs were withdrawn by 1995, the South Western Division being the last to keep them in service. I have many memories of the EPBs as they worked the local lines where I lived in Bromley and later near West Wickham. I travelled to work in London and Croydon in them from 1961 until my marriage in 1968, the little trundle along the line from Elmers End to Addiscombe being particularly noteworthy. Well, anything was better than the dreaded 54 bus! Some of the drivers used to really thrash them on the semi fast peak hour services to and from London, and not only to recover lost time. They were incredibly reliable and I cannot recall any failures in service which affected me. One SR design 4 EPB, one SR design 2 EPB and two BR design 2 EPBs, plus a number of individual vehicles, were preserved.

24 August 1986. 4 EPB 5173 at Charing Cross with the 1315 to Tonbridge. Despite the time the headcode hasn't yet been set. The platforms are deserted and rubbish is evident on the track.

I took very few shots of EPBs on the Western Division but here is 5116 near Boxhill on the 1142 Waterloo to Dorking on 27 October 1982.

Three years earlier on 27 November 1979, BR Design 4 EPB 5339 'built in 1957' is seen leaving Bookham on the 1412 Waterloo to Effingham Junction. The crossover 'incredibly' is hand worked but looks little used.

I managed quite a few EPB shots on the Central section and here we see the doyen of the class, 5001 'built in 1951 to Southern Railway design' at London Bridge working the 1734 to Sutton on a warm 10 August 1983. The beautiful overall roof would last another thirty years and the modern station bears no resemblance to the old one in this scene. The home-going commuters would be happily unhindered by mobile phones or the Internet.

Another scene now completely transformed is West Croydon where 2 EPB 6310 is on the 1409 to Wimbledon on 25 April 1985. This service is now part of Croydon Tramlink which has its stop outside the station. Unit 6310 was originally built to Southern Railway 1951 design in November 1959 using 2 NOL underframes and originally numbered as 5668 and renumbered in January 1984.

This shot is taken at Selsdon on 21 April 1983 and shows 2 EPB 5718 on the 0857 shuttle to Elmers End. Selsdon station no longer exists though the Croydon Tramlink uses much of the route to Elmers End. 5718 was one of the original two-car units built to BR design between 1954 and 1958.

Finally on the Central Division, on a beautiful warm 30 September 1982, 4 EPB 5113 is seen at Norbury on the 1435 Victoria to Sutton. This unit was one of a batch of 213 built to Southern Railway design between 1951 and 1957.

All remaining shots of EPBs are taken on the South Eastern Division where I was most familiar with them. First we have a typical mid-1980s scene at Charing Cross with 4 EPB unit 5173 on the 1315 to Tonbridge and 5454 on the 1308 to Orpington. It was formed in 1983 from 1951 series stock and from other units. This shot was taken on 24 August 1986.

London Bridge at 1706 on 10 August 1983. EPBs 5302, still in all blue, 5048 and 5727 approaching on the 1633 Dartford to Charing Cross, while on the left an EPB heads a down train.

How I remember them best from my many trips to Victoria from Bromley South. Here EPBs 5110 and 5140 approach Beckenham Junction with the 1106 Victoria to Orpington, headcode 70. The date is 9 May 1985.

Bickley has been a much frequented place over the years and here on 3 July 1983 4 EPB 5193 is working the 1125 Victoria to Sevenoaks via Swanley. This train had operated via the Catford loop line.

The next two shots were taken from the footbridge on the London side of Orpington, adjacent to the car sheds. Here on 26 April 1986, 2 EPB 6207 (renumbered from 5707) and refurbished 5475 are approaching with the 0906 from Victoria which will terminate there. The train is on the down fast line but will cross over to use the up bay platform (see next picture). Approaching on the down slow line is the 0910 from Charing Cross which will terminate in the down bay platform.

Seven minutes later at 0950, carrying the incorrect headcode 8 instead of 4, EPB 5150 is unusually leading an 8 CEP formation on the 0744 Ramsgate to Charing Cross. The 0910 from Charing Cross stands in the down bay and EPBs 5475 and 6207 are leaving the up bay forming the 0950 to Victoria. Four more EPB units are stabled. Orpington was indeed the place to be to see these units in the mid-1980s.

Moving down the line to the site of Polhill Box, EPB 5050 is caught arcing while on the 0716 Sevenoaks to Cannon Street. It's just after dawn on a very cold and misty 31 October 1980 and I was there to photograph 33.043 working the penultimate up *Night Ferry*.

Hildenborough bank on 4 July 1985. EPBs 5147 and 5154 are on the 1607 Tonbridge to Holborn Viaduct. They have just passed VEP 7771 working the 1530 Charing Cross to Margate.

On a sunny 3 February 1979, EPB 5240 is seen leaving Paddock Wood on the 1323 Ashford to Charing Cross semi fast service. It was unusual to see non toilet stock on these workings though few people would have been on the train for the whole of the 75 minute journey, as faster services would have been available. On the left is the Paddock Wood shunter 09.011 resting between its duties of sorting Transfesa stock.

On the branch from Paddock Wood and still in all blue, EPB 5213 stands at Maidstone West on the 1600 Paddock Wood to Strood on 1 July 1983. I lived in Paddock Wood for many years and worked in Maidstone from 1974 to 1989, normally using the branch for the commute. I would have been on my way home from work when I took this shot.

Maidstone West was also where SR Utility vans were stabled during the day after bringing in post and parcels in the early morning. Here on 15 June 1983 we see S264, S276 and S375 in the up bay. On the right is the site of the Tuesday market and hidden behind the vans is The Railway Bell public house which was the venue for many slide shows in one of the bars especially closed for us participants. The friendly landlord would also provide a buffet to go with the Shepherd Neame beer which oiled the evening's proceedings. Happy days.

Further towards Strood from Maidstone West is Aylesford where there were some lovely semaphore signals. Here on 2 September 1983 EPB 5156 is on the 1659 Charing Cross to Maidstone West.

At Strood the line from Paddock Wood joined the North Kent line from Charing Cross to the Medway Towns via Dartford. On 13 April 1984 EPBs 5196 and 5027 emerge from the 2.25 mile long Higham and Strood tunnel at Higham with the 1527 Gillingham to Charing Cross.

Turning round I couldn't resist a shot of the immaculate 5027 on the rear of the 1527 Gillingham to Charing Cross. BR blue and BR blue and grey had an absolutely rich sparkling lustre when recently applied, clean and in strong light, but when weathered, dirty and on a dull day it looked dreary and washed out.

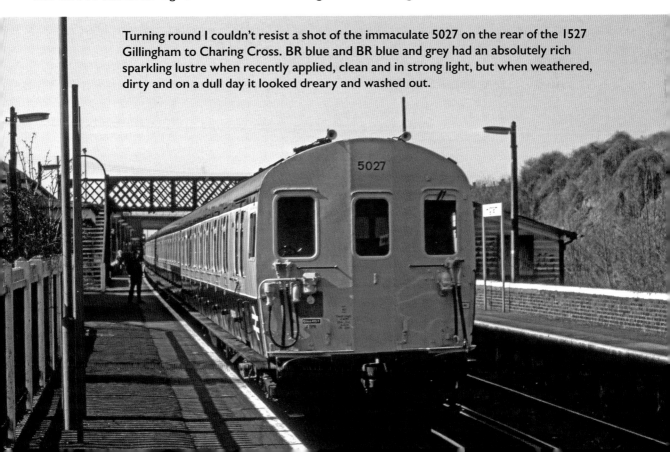

Now in the Medway Towns proper at Chatham on 12 October 1984, EPBs 5111 and 5034 are working the 1348 Charing Cross to Gillingham. On the extreme right can be seen the bus shelters of the then new Chatham Bus/Rail Interchange. This was one of my projects when I worked for Kent County Council and was one of the first in Kent to have traffic lights called by buses. It was also the scene of a very public and loud confrontation with the local planning officer who did not like the idea at all. It was built though, and survives to this day.

2 HAP
1951 SR design stock (Class 414/2) 6001-6042
1957 BR design stock (Class 414/3) phase 1
6043-6105, phase 2 but with phase 1 design
cabs 6106-6146, phase 2 6147-6173

2 SAP
1951 SR design stock 5604-5635
1957 BR design stock 5901-5942

4 CAP
Class 413/2 3201-3213, Class 413/3 3301-3311

Technically similar to the EPBs but with express gearing, these units had first class compartments and were used on all three divisions on main line stopping services and on Coastway work. The 5604-5635 series were to Southern Railway design on underframes built in 1934-36 for 2 NOL units. Due to changing demand and service patterns at times some 2 HAPs had their first class accommodation declassified with the unit becoming second class only and redesignated and renumbered as 2 SAP (Second class HAP). The folding arm rests in the first class compartments were sewn up

into the backrests but this was either not consistently done or passengers unpicked the sewing as armrests were often in use in the then second class compartments. However, with subsequent changes the downgrading was reversed. The 4 CAPs were four-coach sets formed from 2 HAPs semi-permanently coupled with their guard's vans in the centre and the two cabs in the centre locked out of use. This was for dedicated Coastway workings (CAP = Coastway HAP) so platform staff consistently knew where the van space would be. However, this utilisation only lasted for two years after which the 4 CAPs were reallocated to the South Eastern Division and they returned to some of their former 2 HAP haunts. My journey to work in Maidstone from Paddock Wood often involved travelling in a HAP unit and a typical run on the nonstop 0851 train is shown here **Table 5** – See Page 74.

The majority of HAPs, thus CAPs, were built with high levels of blue asbestos, so withdrawal and safe disposal began in late 1982 and within four years they were all gone, except for the ten driving motor brake vehicles rebuilt as Gatwick Luggage Vans (GLVs), and amongst a few other surviving vehicles a complete 2HAP unit is part of the National Collection, It is currently being restored by the Network SouthEast Society as 'Project Commuter'.

4 March 1976. HAP 6080 has just left Paddock Wood with the 0820 Maidstone West to Tonbridge. This shot was taken from the main Tunbridge Wells to Maidstone Road.

A few minutes later on the same day and having crossed the road to face the other way, I caught HAP 6070 leading another HAP on the 0845 Tonbridge to Maidstone West. I sometimes caught this train to work and it was nonstop from Paddock Wood. In the background are the cottages and Oasthouses of Whetsted and just visible is a VEP unit on the 0816 Ashford to Cannon Street service. My notebook tells me that this shot was taken with my Praktica 35 mm camera with Kodachrome 25 slide film exposed at 1/500 of a second at F3.5.

On a very hot 29 July 1983 HAP 6156 brings up the rear of a mixed livery six-coach set on the 1603 Charing Cross to Ramsgate at Whetsted just west of Paddock Wood.

4 CAP 3201 passes Paddock Wood on 3 November 1984 on a down empty stock working to Chart Leacon. The shot is taken from the up side car park where I would take my young children to watch trains.

Moving east of Paddock Wood and into the hopfields of the Garden of England we see a 6 HAP formation led by 6106 on the 1628 Charing Cross to Margate via Canterbury West on 2 September 1980. While this section between Tonbridge and Ashford is largely straight it is far from level. The change in gradient from 1-in-220 down to 1-in-500 up at milepost 35¾ can clearly be seen.

Facing the other way from the previous shot, HAP 6148 is leading CEP 7177 on the 1223 Ashford to Charing Cross train on 16 January 1982. A slow thaw had set in after a severe spell of weather that had seen temperatures as low as -2 centigrade daytime maximum in the Weald of Kent.

Moving now to the London area, next to Orpington carriage sheds we see CAP 3308 leading EPB 5339 on the 0947 empty stock working from Cannon Street to Tonbridge.

With the somewhat austere background belying some quaint streets below, CAP units 3306 and 3203 enter Rochester station with the 1503 Gillingham to Holborn Viaduct service on 12 October 1984. I must have travelled by bus from Maidstone to Chatham that day as my notes state that I caught the 1502 Chatham to Rochester in CAP 3204 coupled to 3204 and 'after taking this picture' the 1536 to Strood in EPB 5301 and finally home on the 1621 to Paddock Wood in CEP 1611.

Travelling a long way east now to the open country at Ospringe west of Faversham, CAP 3207 is on the 1044 Ramsgate to Charing Cross stopping service on 23 October 1984.

Even further east now to Canterbury East and its unusual signal box on 10 June 1985. CAP 3212 plus another CAP unit are on the 1516 Dover Priory to Victoria train. I had arrived from Dover in CEP 1562 on the 1500 fast service.

I have very few shots of HAPs or CAPs on the Central or Western divisions but here is 3209 on the East Coastway 1211 Brighton to Ore service bound for Hastings passing Bo Peep Junction (named after the public house on the A259 below). 6L 1034 waits in the platform at West St Leonards with the 1145 from Charing Cross, 1 May 1984. While in blue and grey livery CAPS retained yellow ends on the intermediate cab fronts, as clearly seen here, but when in Network SouthEast livery intermediate cab fronts were painted black, plus the NSE stripes were not upswept mid unit.

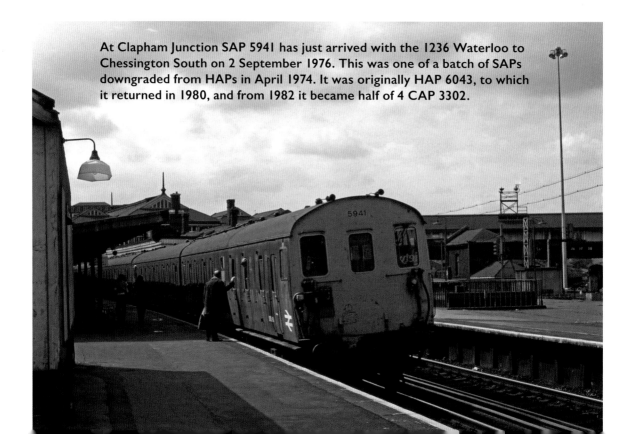

At Clapham Junction SAP 5941 has just arrived with the 1236 Waterloo to Chessington South on 2 September 1976. This was one of a batch of SAPs downgraded from HAPs in April 1974. It was originally HAP 6043, to which it returned in 1980, and from 1982 it became half of 4 CAP 3302.

4 BEPs 7001-7022 Class 410/412. 4 CEPs 7101-7211 Class 411

Six prototype Express units, 7101-7104 and 7001/2, were introduced in 1956 with 1951 electrical equipment and express gearing. CEP for Corridor EPB and BEP for Buffet EPB were first put into service on the Central Division. Further batches with 1957 electrical equipment followed from 1958 to 1963, initially for Phase One of the Kent Coast electrification scheme and seven for the South Western Division. Unit 7153 was rebuilt in 1975 with a revised formation and the remainder followed in due course. The SW units were quickly transferred to the SE and thereafter were concentrated on the South Eastern and Central Divisions where they proved to be very speedy on the faster services, though rough riding until fitted with Commonwealth bogies. In the early 1980s they were renumbered into the series 1501-1620 (CEPs) and 2301-2307 (BEPs) and some were temporarily (for about four years) reformed into four-car formations as 4 TEPs with a

non-refurbished buffet car replacing the second class trailer to cover the 4 BIG refurbishment programme. I travelled home from work in London to Ashford for many years, mainly on the 1710 from Cannon Street which was allowed just 62 minutes with one stop at Tonbridge. It was an 8 CEP, 4 BEP formation with the buffet car attendants serving City gents in their 1st class compartments. This train was nearly always on time or early into Ashford. It was on this train that I timed many very good runs, sometimes with the drivers ignoring the 90 mph speed limit in order to make up time. **Table 6** – *See Page 75.* They finished their days in 2004/5 on the South Eastern increasingly as 3 CEPs (with the trailer standard removed) to be able to work to new Class 375 schedules, and on the South Western Division where some were modified as Greyhound CEPs with an extra stage of field weakening. It was on the SW Division that I timed one at 100 mph. In the period covered by this book all my shots of CEPs are on the South Eastern Division. Three complete CEPS were preserved along with around a dozen individual CEP vehicles.

Bickley cutting on 1 August 1982. 7106 is leading a 12 CEP formation on the 1123 Victoria to Ramsgate. The second unit has been refurbished with the guard's brake moved to the second coach from the end power cars of the unit.

Another shot taken on 1 August but this time in 1984 and at the site of Polhill signal box on the climb from Sevenoaks to the tunnel. Here 1612 leads an eight-car CEP formation on the 1520 Folkestone Harbour to Victoria relief Boat train service which connected with the ferry from Boulogne Maritime and the 1037 from Paris Nord.

The other side of Sevenoaks is the 1-in-122 of Hildenborough bank where down trains could reach very high speeds (see the train running log on page 75) On 25 April 1986 CEPs 1581 and 1563 are on the 1225 Charing Cross to Dover Priory seen at Nizels from the Philpots Lane bridge. I was really there to photograph the Hastings Diesels in their last few weeks but couldn't resist this shot.

Three CEPs together at Ashford on 10 June 1985. 1572 is the rear unit on the 1322 stopping service to Charing Cross, the front unit being 1589, and 1617 is on an ecs working. The 1322 left at 1339 after Ashford had become congested with trains and the signalers took a while to sort things out.

Three CEPs again, this time at Tonbridge with a Hastings 6S on 6 August 1985. From the right 1531 is leading the 0925 Dover Priory to Charing Cross while the 0940 Dover Western Docks to Victoria Boat train is led by 1526. This boat train connected with the 0830 Jetfoil from Oostende which in turn had connections from Belgium and Luxemburg. Unit 1007 is on the 0945 Charing Cross to Hastings. In the down bay is a CEP in early Jaffa Cake colours.

In the period covered by this book the line from Maidstone West to Strood was still mechanically signaled and most stations had semaphore signals. On 11 October 1984 after CEPs had taken over much of the service, 1617 is seen at Snodland with the 1349 Strood to Maidstone West.

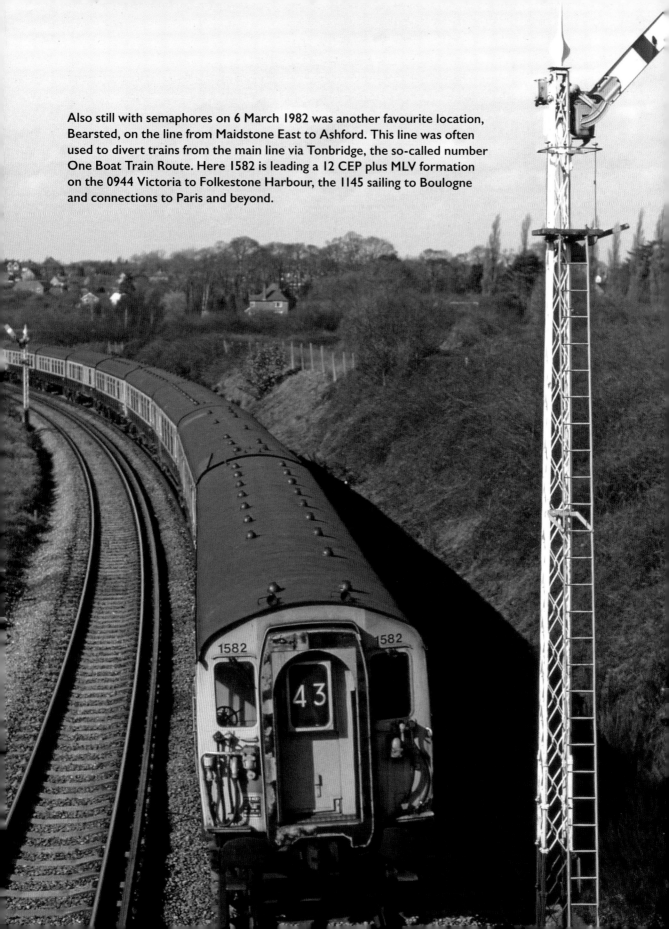

Also still with semaphores on 6 March 1982 was another favourite location, Bearsted, on the line from Maidstone East to Ashford. This line was often used to divert trains from the main line via Tonbridge, the so-called number One Boat Train Route. Here 1582 is leading a 12 CEP plus MLV formation on the 0944 Victoria to Folkestone Harbour, the 1145 sailing to Boulogne and connections to Paris and beyond.

On the same day, CEP 7144 leading a VEP is on the diverted 0912 Margate to Charing Cross service, though the headcode is less than helpful.

As a contrast on a sunny and warm 31 July 1984, CEP 1515 (carrying the little-used 411 prefix) leading a VEP is on the 1536 Margate to Victoria. An even greater contrast at this location is with the shot of CEPs in a blizzard in the section on severe weather on page 176.

The next station east is Hollingbourne and here 1572 is heading a 12 CEP formation on the diverted 1520 Victoria to Ramsgate. On 20 April 1986 I was there to photograph the diverted Hastings Diesels and the VSOE Pullman so the main line via Tonbridge was also closed in addition to that via Chatham. Fortunately neither the M20 nor HS1 have spoilt this view.

Just a short walk from home and on a lovely warm September afternoon, CEPs 1542 and 1612 are seen passing Paddock Wood at speed on the 1510 Dover Priory to Charing Cross. I spent a couple of hours here taking shots with my Bronica ETR-C 6x4.5 camera using Kodak Ectachrome 64 asa slide film. 8 September 1985.

Just east of Paddock Wood was a footbridge, much frequented by myself. Here on 15 December 1984 is a twelve-car CEP formation headed by 1615 on the 1055 fast service from Charing Cross to Ramsgate, first stop Ashford after Waterloo. The new 60 mph crossover from the up fast to the platform road has just been laid and this would save over half a minute for trains stopping at Paddock Wood. This shot was taken with my superb Tamron 135 mm prime lens which is still in use today with my digital cameras.

Two years later the new crossover has completely bedded in as on Christmas Eve 1986 CEP 1545 in late Jaffa Cake livery is passing on a down special working to Ramsgate. A few minutes later 47.500 would pass at high speed with the 1045 Dover Western Docks to Liverpool. (see Page 145). The benign weather would soon give way to one of the worst Januarys ever seen in the UK. See Severe Weather section.

The next station east of Paddock Wood is Marden and here a footbridge crossed the line from the Church and also linked to the staggered platforms. On 6 September 1985 CEPs 1514 and 1504 are on the 1425 Dover Priory to Charing Cross service.

A few miles further on is Staplehurst and near here on 2 September 1980 is refurbished CEP 7153 leading a BEP and a VEP on the 0900 Charing Cross to Ramsgate. 7153 was the first unit to be refurbished and reformed as a trial in 1975 and the other units followed from late 1979. Trial refurbishment is readily distinguishable by sliding ventilator windows rather than the hoppers of the production build. It retained its original window frames.

Over on the north Kent line and on a beautifully warm 1 June 1985, CEPs 1579 and 1619 are on the 1220 Victoria to Ramsgate at Ospringe, just west of Faversham.

At Faversham station on 21 October 1985 CEP 1542 is on the 1050 Victoria to Dover Western Docks. At that time the fast services from Victoria didn't divide at Faversham but ran as complete trains to either Ramsgate or Dover with different stopping patterns in the Medway Towns. The word fast is a misnomer though as the train would take no less than 106 minutes for the 78½ miles.

The area around Faversham Station and indeed the town itself was fascinating with much of interest. This shot taken on 11 March 1982 shows an amazing survivor, a double semaphore signal on the Faversham Creek branch, closed as early as 1964 though the signal box still contains levers. In the background is part of the old steam shed, in front of which is the line to and from Ramsgate, and spanning all lines behind is a footbridge which still exists today.

A beautiful view on the Ashford to Maidstone East line taken in a late afternoon of Sunday, 23 October 1983. With Charing Hill in the background CEP 411512 heads the diverted Ramsgate to Charing Cross service carrying the incorrect headcode, which was for a Cannon Street train.

All remaining shots in the section are taken on the main line to Folkestone and Dover via Tonbridge and Ashford, also known as the No.1 Boat Train Route. On a wintery 11 February 1978 the classic boat train formation of 12 CEP headed by 7194 plus MLV is seen here at Whetsted west of Paddock Wood on the 1344 Victoria to Dover Marine (as it was then) service which connected with the 1615 sailing to Oostende for Belgium and destinations to Germany and Austria including The Tauern Express. Passengers would have to suffer 4 hours 50 minutes on one of the small Belgium Marine ferries on which during an extended six hour crossing in a force 9 gale I felt sea sick for the only time in over two hundred crossings to date.

East of Headcorn at Biddenden Green on the bitterly cold (minus 3 centigrade) 5 January 1985, CEP 1572 is leading another CEP on the 1005 Charing Cross to Ashford service.

Ashford station on 6 March 1974. CEP 7131 has just arrived on the 0900 from Charing Cross. In the background is an unidentified class 71 and the Parish Church looks over the old market town, now much transformed. I travelled in this unit to Dover Priory, changing there to catch CEP 7161 to Dover Marine and then the 1300 sailing to Oostende on the dreaded *Reine Astrid* for the 1657 Oostende-Wien Express and a trip to Austria for steam and trams.

On 5 May 1984 Ashford down sidings yard contain CEP 1578, VEP 7775, HAP 6112, 47.014 and a snowplough.

The day before, on 4 May 1984, CEP 1617 is working with VEP 7889 on the combined 1230 Charing Cross to Margate and 1236 Victoria to Ramsgate seen here leaving Wye on the line from Ashford via Canterbury West. I travelled back to Ashford in a ten-coach formation comprising HAP 6171, VEP 7871 and EPB 5172! Although there appeared to be some disruption to services that day, earlier I had noted the 1200 from Charing Cross arriving at Ashford at 1254, i.e. 7 minutes early and in a time of no more than 51 minutes for the 55.3 miles from Waterloo.

On 10 October 1974 CEP 7182 heading 8 CEP on the 1510 Ramsgate to Cannon Street at Smeeth, four miles east of Ashford.

Slightly further east is Newington Peene. Here on a very cold 9 January 1985, CEPs 1523 and 1544 are on the 1025 Charing Cross to Dover Priory running 25 minutes late. The scene is untroubled by HS1 and the M20 motorway is empty of traffic. Apparently only this hardy photographer was out to record the scene.

Just west of Sandling on the same day CEPs 1599 and 1579 have just passed under the new M20 link road on the 1229 Ramsgate to Charing Cross running just six minutes late.

Folkestone Central station on 29 April 1977. CEP 7127 is on the rear of the 1300 Charing Cross to Ramsgate with 7200 leading. We had travelled down from Paddock Wood in VEP 7860.

From Folkestone Central the line crosses a viaduct above the town and then passes the sidings at Folkestone East, where the boat trains used to reverse before dropping down to the Harbour (see sections on class 33s and 73s). Then comes Martello tunnel after which the line is in Folkestone Warren. Here on 27 August 1985 CEP 1512 is leading Jaffa Cake livery 1602 on the 1155 Charing Cross to Ramsgate. The engineers siding in the foreground no longer exists.

Turning round to face Dover is a beautiful cliff and seascape vista with the 1 mile 182 yard long Abbotscliffe tunnel in the distance. CEPs 1513 and 1505 are on the 1325 Dover Priory to Charing Cross service.

Journey's end for many services was Dover Marine and here on 6 March 1974 is CEP 7161 on the 1130 to Victoria via Canterbury East and the Medway Towns. This station was the starting point of many trips to Europe for steam in the 1970s. This time we were off to Austria.

By the time this shot was taken on 11 June 1985 Dover Marine had been renamed Western Docks (on 14 May 1979). CEP 1531 had arrived earlier and on the right are VEPs 7890, 7773 and 7857 on the 1052 to Victoria which I caught to Canterbury East. It ran the 15.50 miles nonstop from Dover Priory in 15 minutes 13 seconds, with a maximum speed of 87 mph at Bekesbourne. When I worked in the Missing and Tracing section at London Bridge in 1964, one of many frequent enquiries was from the station master here asking about one of the batches of mushroom spawn which was overdue at its destination.

Finally in this section on CEPs is a shot which shows them how I remember them best; on a bright spring day in the hop fields of Kent. 1578 heading an 8 CEP formation on the 1100 fast service from Charing Cross to Ramsgate at Queen Street just east of Paddock Wood. 5 March 1983.

Motor Luggage Vans 68001-68010 Class 419. Renumbered 9001-9010

Built in 1959-61 to provide extra luggage space on the South Eastern boat trains, these vans had two motor traction motors plus batteries and could work on non-electrified lines using battery power. They were withdrawn from boat train service in 1991/92 with the closure of Dover Western Docks, but they went on to have a second career as departmental vehicles

with the last one remaining in service with South West Trains at Bournemouth Depot until 2004. Most MLVs have remarkably been preserved. For a time, six standard brake vehicles (BGs) were adapted for multiple unit working and numbered 68201-68206, designated TLV (Trailer Luggage Van), but were unpowered. They increased a full boat train consist to fourteen coaches. All were withdrawn in 1975, but they also went on to have careers as departmental coaches.

On 10 August 1985 MLV 68010 is heading
a 12 CEP formation on the 1505 Folkestone
Harbour to Victoria up Hildenborough
bank at Nizels.

Paddock Wood on 28 October 1983. MLV 68007 leads the standard 12 CEP formation on the 1340 Dover Western Docks to Victoria. This connected with the classic ferry sailing at 1005 from Oostende. On the extreme left is the Transfesa depot with its many sidings and across the other side of the line to Maidstone West is Pascual's depot. Both dealt primarily with fruit from Spain.

Jaffa Cake liveried 9005 leading a 12 CEP formation through Ashford on 26 August 1987 on the 1535 Folkestone Harbour to Victoria service, connecting from the ferry from Calais.

A scene transformed beyond recognition by HS1 is this one at Westenhanger on 25 April 1976. It was a pleasant spot where we could spend the hours quietly photographing trains. MLV 68002 brings up the rear of a 12 CEP formation on the 1030 Victoria to Folkestone Harbour train which was the main morning service to Paris via Boulogne and the successor to the Golden Arrow which had ceased on 30 September 1972.

In very different conditions and slightly further east near Sandling on 9 January 1985, MLV 68006 heads the usual 12 CEP formation on the 1255 Dover Western Docks to Victoria. The MLV always led in the up direction to assist speedy unloading at Victoria.

The MLVs had a number of workings away from boat trains and here we see 68005 at Chatham on the 1353 Victoria to Dover Western Docks on 12 October 1984. It was trailing an 8 VEP formation.

Tables

Table 3

EPBs- EAST CROYDON TO LONDON BRIDGE

Run No.	1813 East Croydon to London Bridge	1755 East Croydon to London Bridge
Date	1 July 1969	15 December 1969
Units	5168+5224	5787+5047+5223
Timed by	Author	Author

	miles	time	mins	secs	speed	miles	time	mins	secs	speed
East Croydon						0.00	0.00	00	00	
Windmill Bridge Jct						0.50		00	51	43
Norwood Junction	0.00	0.00	00	00		1.67		02	12	56
MP 8¼	0.44		00	52	43	2.11		02	40	57½
Anerley	1.10		01	37	55½	2.77		03	19	60
Penge West	1.50		02	02	61	3.17		03	42	64
Sydenham	2.19		02	42	65	3.86		04	22	67½
Forest Hill	3.06		03	25	68	4.73		05	05	69½
MP 5½	3.19		03	32	70	4.86		05	13	70
Honor Oak Park	3.95		04	08	76	5.62		05	50	76
MP 4	4.69		04	43	80	6.36		06	24	80
Brockley	4.99		04	55	82	6.66		06	35	82
MP 3½	5.19		05	05	83½	6.86		06	46	83
New Cross Gate	5.81		05	31	85	7.48		07	14	75*
Bricklayers Arms Jct	6.51		06	10	64*	8.18		08	27	26* sigs
Spa Road	7.54		07	04	60	9.21		09	52	47
								sigs stop		0*
London Bridge	8.69	12.00	09	12		10.36	14.00	16	28	
	slow finish into platform 10 equivalent time with finish to platform 14=8 mins 45 secs					net time 10 mins 45 secs personal fastest time to pass New Cross Gate				

Table 4

4 EPBs WATERLOO TO WIMBLEDON

Train			1222 Waterloo to Guildford (New Line)				1222 Waterloo to Guildford (New Line)		
Date			7 March 1966				20 May 1966		
Unit			5248				5307		
Timed by			Author				Author		

	miles	sched	mins	secs	speed	sched	mins	secs	speed
Waterloo	0.00	0.00	00	00		0.00	00	00	
Vauxhall	1.29		02	25	44½		02	14	50
Loco Jct	2.35		03	26	59½		03	14	56½
Queens Road	2.81		03	54	61		03	42	64
Clapham Junction	3.93	6.00	05	20	47*	6.00	05	00	40*
Milepost 5	5.00		06	37	53½		06	20	55
Earlsfield	5.58		07	15	60		06	55	63
Durnsford Road	6.31		07	58	62		07	37	64
Wimbledon	7.24	10.30	09	09		10.30	08	48	
	Note the incredibly fast starts compared with what is normal today								

Table 5

Train		0851 Paddock Wood to Maidstone West
Date		6 January 1976
Units		2 HAP No. 6150
Timed by		Author

	miles	sched	mins	secs	speed
Paddock Wood	0.00	0.00	00	00	
Beltring	1.81		02	37	63½/65
Yalding	3.44		04	19	52*
Wateringbury	5.17		06	15	54
Teston LC	6.44		07	20	60/26* tsr
East Farleigh	8.11		10	02	38/49
Maidstone West	9.95	15.00	12	53	
	net time 12 minutes				

Table 6

Train	1710 Cannon Street to Ashford
Date	18 June 1969
Units	7160+7013+7134
Load	12 coaches, 3,000 HP, 445 tons tare, 480 tons gross
Timed by	Author

	miles	sched	mins	secs	speed
Cannon Street	0.00	0.00	00	00	
			sigs		3*
London Bridge	0.71	2.00	02	50	30
New Cross	3.68		06	44	61
St Johns	4.42	6.00	07	33	50*
			sigs		29*
Parks Bridge jct	5.01		08	30	40
Hither Green	6.03	9.00	09	41	54
Grove Park	7.81		11	30	57
Elmstead Woods	9.09		12	53	58
Chistlehurst	10.07	14.00	13	50	62
Petts Wood	11.52		15	07	64
Orpington	12.64	17.00	16	09	67
			pws		30*
Chelsfield	14.14		17	39	17*
			pws		18*
Knockholt	15.38		20	27	43
Polhill Tunnel North	16.08		21	17	56
Polhill Tunnel South	17.53		22	57	74
Polhill Box (site)	18.03		23	19	78
Dunton Green	19.41		24	22	83
Sevenoaks	20.94	25.30	25	30	73
Sevenoaks Tunnel North	21.48		25	54	70
Sevenoaks Tunnel South	23.48		27	19	84
Weald Box	23.93		27	52	87
MP 26	24.83		28	28	90
Hildenborough	25.86		29	07	96
MP 28	26.83		29	45	93
Tonbridge	28.56	33.00	31	50	
	Net time: 27mins 15secs		* brakes or speed restriction		
	Timed from front power car				

CHAPTER THREE

1963 ELECTRIC MULTIPLE UNIT STOCK

4 BIGs 7031-7058 Class 420/422. 4 CIGs 7301-7438 Class 421

4 VEPs 7701-7894 Class 423

The CIGs entered service in 1964/65 on the Central Division, replacing the original Brighton and Eastbourne stock. CIG = Corridor Brighton Stock as IG was the LB&SCRly code for Brighton, although the abbreviation is also attributed to Corridor Intermediate Guard. Later new types of units were also corridor intermediate guard designs but the CIGs came first. They had four EE507 traction motors, rated at 250 hp, for the first time fitted to the intermediate brake vehicle, and a top speed of 90 mph. A further batch was delivered from 1970 to replace the 4 COR stock on the Portsmouth direct line and in 1971/72 to replace the CORs on the Central Division. I have very few photos of these units in the period covered by this book, though in their later days on the Western Division I obtained more shots. I regarded the Greyhound versions with an extra stage of field weakening as probably the finest traditional type of Southern Region unit ever produced. They were extremely reliable and in one four-week control

period they returned a figure of infinity for delays in service caused by technical faults, i.e. there weren't any. As far as I know this has never happened before or since with any rolling stock on the railway system. A number of complete 4 CIGs and individual CIG vehicles have been preserved.

Electrically the VEPs (Vestibule EPBs) were almost identical to the 1970 CIGs but with 275 hp EE507 traction motors. This meant that they had the edge in acceleration and top speed compared to the non-Greyhound CIGs and it showed in normal service. **Table 7** – *See Page 85.* The official top speed allowed was still 90 mph though. They were intended for semi fast and outer suburban work with high density second class seating and doors at each bay so could be drafty and uncomfortable. They were worked regularly on long distance services, and worked on all three divisions. The VEPs were derided by both passengers and enthusiasts, however they did an unglamorous job efficiently and loyally over many years, arguably more comfortable than modern EMUs now in use. One complete 4 VEP, 3417, was preserved by South West Trains and is now owned by the Bluebell Railway in the care of the Southern Traction Group. A number of other VEP vehicles remain.

Bo Peep Junction is where the Central Division East Coastway lines meet those of the South Eastern Division from Charing Cross via Tunbridge Wells and could be photographed from the platforms at West St Leonards on the latter line. Here on 3 May 1984 CIG 7304 brings up the rear of the 0853 Victoria to Ore service. Signal sighting through the long tunnel to Warrior Square must have been difficult.

Through the tunnel to Warrior Square and after another, shorter tunnel is Hastings. On 25 May 1984 BIG 7046 is leading CIG 7310 on the 1130 to Victoria via Eastbourne. By that date the semaphore signaling had been partially replaced but the signals at the far end of the station remain to this day. In the background is Emmanuel Church on West Hill. Hastings is a fascinating place, especially the old town, and I spent some years there working on regeneration projects.

On 26 July 1985 NSE ran a special train for the press and other interested parties at 1026 from Victoria to Brighton. Refurbished CIG 1701 in Jaffa Cake livery was used and is seen here at Redhill contrasting with CIG 7431, one of the second batch built in 1971/1972 to replace 4 COR units on the Central Division. It was a low key occasion though it made for a nice day out courtesy of NSE.

Over on the South Western Division CIG 1224 is leading another CIG at speed near Newnham Siding east of Basingstoke on 27 September 1987, working the 0858 Bournemouth to Waterloo semi fast service.

CIG units didn't get to the South Eastern Division until after the period covered by this book but the division had the majority of the 4 VEP units. On 22 October 1985 7866 sits at Maidstone East with the 1225 Victoria to Margate. Another VEP unit is in the bay platform while County Hall presides over the scene. Despite working for Kent County Council for fifteen years I was never based there.

On a beautiful 1 June 1985, Unit 7761 is seen approaching Chartham west of Canterbury on the 0925 Victoria to Margate.

A few weeks earlier on 6 May 1985, 7864 leaves Selling with the 1453 Victoria to Dover Western Docks. At that time east Kent still had a great deal of semaphore signaling which I tried to include in my photographs whenever possible.

On the South Eastern Division this scene is just south of Polhill Tunnel and shows 7775 leading another VEP on the 1625 Charing Cross to Ramsgate on 1 August 1984.

To complete the set of 7864-7866 with 7865 we see it here at one of my favourite locations just west of Paddock Wood working the 1330 Ashford to Charing Cross semi fast service on 6 March 1976. This train would have been combined at Tonbridge with the 1210 from Margate. In the background another VEP can just be seen running into the station with the 1310 Charing Cross to Ashford train.

A few weeks earlier on 9 February 1976, 7856 is on the 1130 Ashford to Charing Cross. This shot is taken from the foot crossing just west of Paddock Wood.

In very different conditions on 6 January 1985, 7883 is arriving at Beltring Halt with the 1021 Paddock Wood to Strood service. The snow was still falling and the mercury stood at zero centigrade.

Three days later on 9 January 1985 and much further east at Sevington, 7872 is running 35 minutes late with the 1225 Charing Cross to Dover Priory. I had driven through deep snow to get to this spot from the A20 trunk road and didn't linger long.

VEPs galore at the old Ashford Station on 28 June 1983. 7882 is on the 1203 from Charing Cross and 7880 with 7772 are on a down empty stock train.

On the line to Canterbury West the first station is Wye and here on 4 May 1984 Unit 7777 is approaching on the 1312 Margate to Charing Cross train. Using an area runabout ticket on that day from Paddock Wood I visited Tonbridge, West St Leonards, Hastings, Ashford, Wye, Hastings again, Battle, Tunbridge Wells, Battle again and finally Tonbridge and back to Paddock Wood. Timekeeping was good all day.

Table

Table 7

Train	1457 Ashford to Charing Cross
Date	5 June 1985
Units	7770+7862
Timed by	Author
Weather	Heavy rain

	miles	mins	secs	speed
Ashford	0.00	00	00	
Chart Siding (site)	2.11	02	39	67
Pluckley	5.67	05	21	87
MP 49	7.11	06	21	85
MP 46	10.11	08	21	94
Headcorn	10.86	08	52	95
MP 43	13.11	10	16	93/94
Staplehurst	14.25	11	03	91
Marden	16.72	12	42	90
MP 38	18.11	13	34	92
Paddock Wood	21.29	16	35	
	Average MP46-MP38:92.02 mph Start to stop average:77.03 mph Timed from rear of train in the dtc of 7862			

CHAPTER FOUR
BOURNEMOUTH STOCK

4 REPs 3001-3015 Class 430/432.
TCs 401-434 Class 491/438

These units, the majority of the vehicles of which were converted from locomotive-hauled coach stock, were introduced in 1967 and a further batch of four 4 REPS (with different types of restaurant cars) in 1974 all for the Bournemouth electrification. The REPs were tractor units with one 400 hp English Electric traction motor on each axle of each motor coach of which there was one at each end of the four-coach unit, so 3,200 HP in total (only 100 HP less than the famed Deltic locomotives) and were therefore very powerful. Three TC (Trailer Car) units were built as three cars designated 3 TC but they were later augmented to 4 TC. Normally they would work with two four-car TC units as far as Bournemouth, where one TC unit would be taken forward to Weymouth by a class 33 diesel loco. When working as REP plus one TC unit the acceleration could be very rapid, far exceeding anything else working on the Southern at that time. I once timed one at 106 mph and it gave me a faster time between Basingstoke and Woking than the best I had in the days of steam, but not by much! Only the class 50 diesel locos could equal this, though the current excellent class 444s can do so on a daily basis as they are allowed 100 mph. A more normal run to Southampton with a REP/TC combination is shown. `Table 8` – *See Page 91.* Speed was officially limited to 90 mph due to braking distances. They were replaced by September 1991 by class 442 electric units. No REP units were preserved but two 4 TC units (not in original formations) and a number of individual TC vehicles have been preserved.

The old train departure indicator board on the main line and suburban side at Waterloo in 1976. It had been there for fifty years but in another year would be gone. Note that queuing was still in vogue then.

Having spent most of the 1960s chasing steam on the Bournemouth line, I hardly went back after steam ended on 9 July 1967. Somehow I didn't want to taint so many sacred memories. On 2 September 1976 though I was at Clapham Junction and photographed the classic immediate post steam formation of 8TC plus REP formation on the 1230 Waterloo to Weymouth headed by TC429. In the days of steam of course this would have been the *Bournemouth Belle* all Pullman car train with passengers for Weymouth catered for by the 1235 from Waterloo.

Also at Clapham Junction, but on 16 April 1980, 33.107 is on a TC set working the 1707 postal workers train from Kensington Olympia.

Exactly eight years later on Network Day, 16 April 1988, 73.132 is heading a train of TC units on the 1000 Bournemouth to Waterloo running 14 minutes late. Another class 73 lurks in the yard. I was then off to London Bridge to record the record time of 319.033 and 319.031 to Brighton in 39 minutes 14 seconds with a maximum speed of 102 mph at Horley. Chris Green, NSE supremo, was on board.

TC units also worked with class 33 diesel locos push-pull on the semi fast services from Waterloo to Salisbury. Here on 10 March 1988, 33.119 is on the 0810 from Waterloo at Pirbright, a spot much favoured in the days of steam. The Salisburys alternated every other hour with the Exeter services hauled by class 50s with early MK2s.

At Old Basing on 19 April 1984 the classic 8TC plus 4REP formation led by 405 is on a Waterloo to Weymouth semi fast service. The TC units were always in the front going down so that one unit could be hauled from Bournemouth to Weymouth by class 33 diesel and then propelled back to connect with the rest of the train at Bournemouth which would have been led by a REP.

Basingstoke on 28 February 1986. REP 3005 is leading TC 418 on the 0900 Bournemouth to Waterloo semi fast. Although limited to 90 mph my highest recorded speed with a REP+ TC formation was 106 mph near Fleet, exactly the same speed and place as my highest speed with Southern steam.

On 27 September 1987, 73.110 is on the 1034 semi fast Weymouth to Waterloo leading two TC units at Worting Junction, two and a half miles west of Basingstoke.

Table

Table 8

Date	14 December 1968
Train	1030 am Waterloo to Weymouth
Loco	Rep 3005 and TC 405
Load	8 coaches, 3,200 HP, 311 tons tare, 335 tons gross
Recorder	Author

	miles	sched	mins	secs	speed	
Waterloo	0.00	0.00	00	00		
Vauxhall	1.29		02	22	44/60	
Clapham Junction	3.93	6.30	05	25	40*/62	
Wimbledon	7.24		10	37	4*	tsr/sigs
New Malden	9.78		13	21	62/51*	sigs
Surbiton	12.04		16	10	60	
Hampton Court Jct	13.34	16.00	17	25	64	
Hersham	15.91		19	30	82	
Walton	17.08		20	20	85	
Weybridge	19.15		21	46	88	
Byfleet and New Haw	20.40		22	38	92	
Woking	24.29	25.00	25	20	87/86	
Brookwood	27.99		27	54	87/89	
MP 31	31.00		29	55	88/94	
Farnborough	33.20		31	22	90/85	
Fleet	36.48		33	39	90/94	
Winchfield	39.83		35	54	86/85	
Hook	42.16		37	31	87	
Basingstoke	47.75		41	38	65*/73	
Worting Jct	50.26	45.00	43	51	60*	
Wootton Box	52.50		45	54	75	
Roundwood Box	56.20		48	31	90/92	
Micheldever	58.05		49	47	90/86	
Wallers Ash Box	61.70		52	17	90/92	
Winchester Jct Box	64.45	56.00	54	03	88/61*	tsr
Winchester	66.55		55	56	86/92	
Shawford	69.61		58	06	88/92	
Eastleigh	73.45	62.30	60	55	60*	
St Denys	77.12		64	0	76	
Northam Jct	78.20	67.00	65	11	14*	
Southampton Central	79.24	70.00	67	43		
	net time 65 minutes					
	* brakes or speed restriction					

CHAPTER FIVE
IOW STOCK

3 TIS 031-036 Class 486. 4VEC 041-046 Class 485

The VEC-TIS units were formed from ex-London Transport stock built between 1923 and 1935 introduced in 1967 to replace steam and to fit the restricted height on the Island lines. They had GEC WT54A 240 HP traction motors. They were replaced from 1989 with ex-London Transport 1938 stock.

I made just one visit to the Isle of Wight during the period covered by this book and that was on 8 August 1983. At Ryde Pier Head 3TIS 036 is on a short working from Esplanade while on the right 4VEC 043 is on the 1310 to Shanklin.

034 and 044 approaching
Sandown on the 1655 Ryde
Pier Head to Shanklin.

035 and 045 leaving Sandown
on the 1702 Shanklin to Ryde
Pier Head.

044 and 034 entering Sandown on the 1721 Shanklin to Ryde Pier Head. The SR Utility vans in the bay platform were static stores vans used by the PW department.

036 at Ryde Pier Head on a short working to Ryde Esplanade.

On 8 August 1983 our journey to and from the Island was in MV Southsea and here the ship is seen approaching Ryde Pier on the 1733 from Portsmouth Harbour. Our journey from there back to Paddock Wood started with VEPs 7756 and 7738 which ran on time and reached 95 mph down the bank after Haslemere.

CHAPTER SIX
DIESEL MULTIPLE UNIT STOCK

6S Class 201 1001-1007, 6L
Class 202 1011-1019 and 6B 1031-1037
Class 203. 3R 1201-1206, Class 206

The six-coach units were introduced in 1957/58 to replace steam on the Charing Cross to Hastings line via Tunbridge Wells. Due to tight clearances in the tunnels at Tunbridge Wells they were 8ft 2½in wide with flat sided bodies. 6S = short (57ft) bodies, 6L = long (63ft 6in) bodies and 6B = long units including a buffet car. Each of the two motor coaches in each unit had an English Electric 4 cylinder type 4SRKT engine feeding generators powering two EE507 250 hp traction motors, giving 1,000 HP per six-coach unit or 2,000 HP for a twelve-coach train as compared to 3,000 HP for a 12 CEP formation. This meant the trains had to be allowed extra time on the main line between London and Tonbridge, especially as they were limited in theory to 75 mph. Performance uphill could be dreary, particularly with two of the heavier 6L units. They were however my favourite class of Southern multiple unit and I have a great number of photographs and train running logs of them. To get an 'even time' start-to-stop run was very unusual and one is shown here, achieved with the help of a complete disregard of the 75 mph limit. Table 9 – *See Page 130.* They could be very rough riding at speed. They were withdrawn when the Hastings line was electrified in May 1986, but one unit, numbered 1001 and formed of various coaches, including normal width MK 1 trailer stock, is preserved and operated by Hastings Diesels Limited and works on the main line from time to time. There was much reforming of the units and in 1965 units 1002-1004 were disbanded and two driving motor brake and trailer second cars from each formed into six three-coach 3R units 1201-1206 each with a modified driving trailer from a 2 EPB unit. The visual effect of two narrow vehicles combined with a wider one gave them their nickname of 'Tadpoles'. They were used on Tonbridge to Reading services, the 'R' from Reading inspiring the unit designation. For some years I travelled home from work in one between Redhill and Tonbridge.

This section covers the Hastings Diesels and starts with 6S 1006 at Charing Cross on the 1345 to Hastings on 22 September 1985. My collection of shots of these iconic units is huge and more than enough to fill a book, let alone one small section of a book about the Southern after the end of steam.

The Hastings units predated the end of steam by ten years of course and I have shots of them from 1960 onwards. This scene by Orpington car sheds shows 6L units 1017 and 1034 on the 0945 Charing Cross to Hastings on 25 April 1986.

A few seconds later and facing the other way, 1011 and 1016 passed at speed on the 0840 Hastings to Charing Cross. My notes say that they were moving at about 80 mph.

Earlier the same day 6L units 1013 and 1012 are seen at Twitton, south of Polhill tunnel, on the 0827 Charing Cross to Hastings. St Leonards depot would often keep consecutively numbered units formed together.

My mission on 25 April 1986 was to photograph the Hastings diesels in as many locations north of Tonbridge as possible in view of their impending demise in May. Also at Twitton from the same bridge as the previous shot, 6L units 1017 and 1034 are running on time on the 0734 Hastings to Cannon Street service. This was the last time the train was worked by Hastings units. It would run empty stock to Charing Cross to turn and form the 0945 down as seen in the previous shot at Orpington. Out of sight and on the right of the train was the site of the old Polhill signal box.

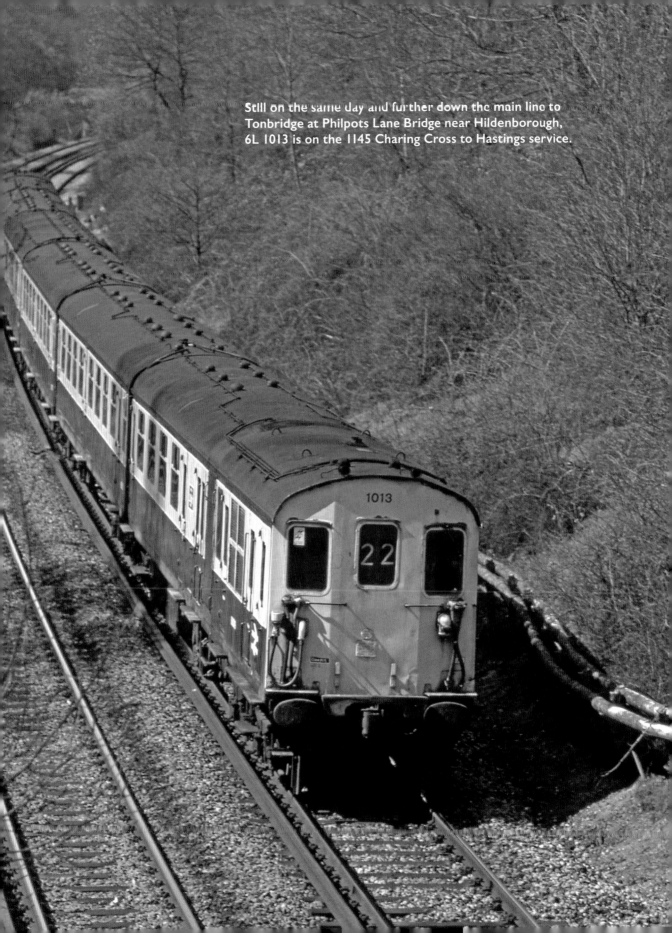

Still on the same day and further down the main line to Tonbridge at Philpots Lane Bridge near Hildenborough, 6L 1013 is on the 1145 Charing Cross to Hastings service.

The next day, 26 April 1986, and from the same bridge but facing towards Tonbridge, 1013 is coupled with 1012 climbing the 1-in-122 with the 1243 Hastings to Charing Cross service.

I am a great lover of low light photography as these next two shots taken at Sevenoaks show. First on 20 November 1984 1007 and 1004 are seen approaching Sevenoaks with the 0828 Charing Cross to Hastings. It was a fine morning after fog had cleared and my notebook suggests that I had gone there specially to get this shot. Unit 1007 was one of those involved in the Hither Green disaster on 5 November 1967, the other being 1017. I missed this by a few hours having travelled up from Tunbridge Wells in the afternoon.

Sevenoaks Station on 21 December 1984 facing south towards the two mile tunnel with the sun just touching trees on the right. 6B unit 1031 and 6L 1014 are working hard on the 0738 Hastings to Cannon Street. Can't you just hear those English Electric SRKT motors? By then 1031 was actually running as a 6L with a trailer second coach from 1032 replacing the buffet car. Hastings Buffet cars were withdrawn in 1980.

6S 1006 seemed to follow me around and so the next two shots show this unit, first arriving at Tonbridge on 6 August 1985 working the 0952 Cannon Street to St Leonards Warrior Square.

Nearly five years earlier on 21 October 1980, 1006 is seen leaving Tonbridge and climbing the 1-in-53 gradient to Somerhill Tunnel at Lavender Hill, another favourite spot of mine through the years. The train is the 1345 Charing Cross to Hastings.

At Tunbridge Wells Central Goods, 6L 1012 is on the 1044 Hastings to Charing Cross on 1 February 1981.

South of Tunbridge Wells is Wadhurst, and leaving here on 7 May 1984 is 1013 on the 1445 Charing Cross to Hastings service. The train was about to enter the 1,205 yard long tunnel which would take the railway into Snape Wood and the long downhill section into the Rother Valley, where high speeds were often recorded.

Climbing through Snape Wood on 12 April 1984 on the 1344 Hastings to Charing Cross is 6L unit 1018. There is a foot crossing at this point which was quite difficult to find from the secluded country lane below.

The next six shots were all taken at or near Etchingham in the Rother Valley and at the foot of descents from both directions. On the semi fast services it was the point where the Hastings units would be travelling at maximum speed. This shot 'also taken on 12 April 1984' shows 6B 1034 with 6L 1018 slowing for the Etchingham stop. 1034 had long since lost its buffet car and was running as a 5L.

The same location but in very different conditions on 12 February 1985 shows 1035 and 1017 on the 0945 Charing Cross to Hastings. The 6B is also running as a 5L.

Nearer to the station and with up trains, the next two shots also show contrasting weather conditions. First in this shot taken on 12 August 1983, 6L 1011 and 6S 1003 are on the 1533 Hastings to Charing Cross train. The temperature that day was 28 degrees centigrade.

On 13 February 1985 at the same location it was minus one degree centigrade as the 1033 Hastings to Charing Cross service leaves with unit 1015.

One of the attractions of Etchingham was the selection of superb semaphore signals and in this shot the up starter guards the section towards Stonegate while sister 6B units 1036 and 1035, running as 5Ls, enter the station with the 1045 Charing Cross to Hastings on 23 May 1984.

The other attraction was the friendly signalman at this relatively remote and quiet location, the village then being no more than a ribbon development of a few houses. On more than one occasion we were invited up into the box to watch train movements and to keep him company. Units 1013 and 1006 have just passed the signal box on the 1245 Charing Cross to Hastings.

From Etchingham the line climbs up past Robertsbridge to Mountfield tunnel and then on to Battle where on 4 May 1984 an immaculate 6L 1011 arrives with the 1445 Charing Cross to Hastings. Unusually the leading edge of the roof and airhorns are yellow!

On the same day 6B 1036 'running as a 6L unit with 6L 1013' arrive with the 1540 Hastings to Cannon Street. It would return at 1736 running fast to Tonbridge and would divide at Tunbridge Wells with 1013 running fast to Robertsbridge then all stations to Hastings and 1036 all stations to Etchingham then fast to West St Leonards, Warrior Square and Hastings, a unique calling pattern that would cease with the timetable change on 14 May.

On the previous day, 3 May 1984, 6B unit 1031 running as a 5L departs from Battle with the 1445 Charing Cross to Hastings.

Moving down the line to West St Leonards where the line from Charing Cross meets the east Coastway line from Eastbourne, 6S 1001 is arriving past a fine array of semaphore signals and Bo Peep signal box with the 1344 Hastings to Charing Cross on 1 May 1984. The Coastway line didn't have platforms here but previously did at West Marina which was closed in 1967. The platforms still exist, albeit very overgrown.

From the junction seen in the previous shot the line runs through a 1,318 yard long tunnel to St Leonards (Warrior Square) station where on 30 July 1985 6S units 1005 and 1004 are seen emerging from the tunnel to Hastings with the 1636 Hastings to Charing Cross service which was running five minutes late here and lost more time to Tonbridge, arriving 12 minutes late due to a number of out-of-course delays.

End of the line at Hastings on 11 May 1986 with unit 6L 1018 on the 1545 from Charing Cross. This was the last day of the Hastings Diesels and my last down run with one of these units in normal service. We had run the 8.14 miles from Wadhurst to Etchingham in 8 minutes 26 seconds with a maximum speed of 88 mph. 1018 with 1013 (with a power car from 1004) then formed the 1743 to Charing Cross which I travelled on as far as Tonbridge.

Unit 1016 is seen waiting for time at Tunbridge Wells on the rear of 1543 Hastings to Charing Cross. I alighted at Tunbridge Wells to catch the 1545 from Charing Cross with units 1018 and 1013. See picture above.

At a minute after 8 pm 1032 and 1002 are seen on the 1918 special from Hastings to Charing Cross. They are going well and are passing VEP 7842 heading the 1923 Ashford to Charing Cross which had arrived early at two minutes to eight. The light was very poor and so I used black and white to secure an acceptable shot. Half an hour later 1018 and 1013 appeared again on the last down Hastings Diesel worked train, the 1945 Charing Cross to Hastings, which left amidst a cacophony of horns and whistles, all of which I have on tape.

During the time that the route from Tunbridge Wells to West St Leonards was being electrified and the narrow tunnels reduced to single track, there were many diversions, mainly via Tonbridge and Ashford to Hastings. Here 6L 1011 is passing Five Oak Green on 7 September 1985 with the 1145 Charing Cross to Hastings.

On the same day and further down the line at Marden, 6B 1031
'running as a 6L' is on the 1401 Hastings to Charing Cross.

The Hastings units also had a regular turn away from their normal main line and this was on the 1615
Tonbridge to Edenbridge school train. In this shot 6B 1035 'running as a 5L' is entering Penshurst.

After the end of their era on the Charing Cross to Hastings line 6L 1011 was reformed as a four-car unit and numbered 203.001 to provide relief for the hard pressed class 205 units on the Ashford to Hastings line. In fact 203.001 had regular turns and here we see the unit leaving Hastings on the 1605 to Ashford on 19 May 1987. The train is leaving the bay platform and passing the superb array of semaphore signals which are still in situ at the time of writing.

Sometime in 1987 I had discovered that 6L 1013, one of my favourite Hastings units, had been renumbered as 202.001 and had a peak hour working from East Grinstead to London Bridge and return and so I determined to find a spare day to cover it. In fact I had a half day off work and travelled from Maidstone West to Strood and Waterloo thence to London Bridge and down to East Croydon where I joined the 1751 back to London Bridge with 202.001 and 205.015. We were somewhat late and reached 73 mph down Brockley bank. Having had my ride I caught the 1814 to New Cross Gate in EPB 5447 and was lucky to secure this shot of 202.001 and 205.105 on the 1823 London Bridge to East Grinstead on a beautiful evening. The date is 29 June 1987.

I didn't get many shots of the 3R 'Tadpole' units but here is one from 26 March 1978. 1203 is at Blackhoath Lane nearing Penshurst with the 1345 Tonbridge to Redhill. For some years I travelled home from work at East Croydon in one of these units on the 1704 from Redhill to Tonbridge. This train connected with the 1646 from East Croydon at Redhill, a five-minute connection made after changing platforms under the subway, and at Tonbridge into the 1710 from Cannon Street, an eight-minute connection made by changing platforms over the footbridge. Needless to say, it always worked. You couldn't even consider making such connections on today's unreliable and disjointed railway of course.

Whereas most numerical headcodes are bi-directional, the Tonbridge–Redhill–Reading route had discrete headcodes for each direction. Reading–Redhill–Tonbridge was 55.

Finally in this section here is the headboard carried by 6L 1018 on the last DEMU worked 1800 Cannon Street to Hastings on 9 May 1986. The train ran well reaching 87 mph down Hildenborough bank.

3H 1101-1133 Class 205. 3T 1401-1404 Class 204 and 3D 1301-1319 Class 207.

Initially built from 1957 as phase 1 design two-coach trains, effectively diesel HAPs, they were later strengthened to three coaches and were used for the Hampshire dieselisation scheme and later for the Ashford to Hastings line. ('H' for Hampshire and later Hastings.) The final batch of seven was built for Salisbury–Reading services.

Although they had larger guard's vans and were to 1957 phase 2 design they were still designated 3H but called 'Berkshire' units. The 3D units, with modern looking reinforced glass fibre cab fronts and narrower Hastings stock width bodies, were built in 1962 for the Oxted line. The 'D' from Oxted giving them their designation. They had similar traction to the Hastings Units and were also limited to 75 mph. They had very long lives and were finally displaced by Turbostars in 2004.

I start the section on the three-coach 3H and 3D diesel units with some shots on the Ashford to Hastings line. 3H 1119 is seen near Kingsnorth on 10 October 1974 on the 1625 Ashford to Hastings. I lived near here until towards the end of 1974 and took quite a few shots; one of many locations in the Ashford area now transformed by development. Units 1119-1122 were introduced in 1958 specifically for Ashford–Hastings services, and while units could be moved around, this unit was on its original home ground at this time.

Sister unit 1120 is seen in the snow at Bromley Green, near Ham Street, on the 1440 Ashford to Hastings on 9 January 1985.

Finally on 30 August 1987 205.101 is approaching Hastings with the 1704 from Ashford. The girder bridge has been replaced but most of the semaphore signals remain.

Moving to London now, the next two shots are at London Bridge on 10 August 1983. This shot shows 1101 and 1123 arriving with empty stock at 1702 to form the 1706 to East Grinstead. In the background is a ten-coach EPB formation on the south eastern side and a CIG unit on the Central Division. Note incorrect use of double red blank blind on the front.

A few minutes earlier all blue 3D 1311 and 3H 1105 are arriving on time with the combined 1510 Uckfield and 1546 East Grinstead. This combination would return at 1736 to Uckfield and East Grinstead, dividing at Oxted. More scenes at London Bridge are in the sections on EPBs and class 33s.

Moving now to the Tonbridge to Eridge line, 3D unit 1314 is at High Brooms with the 0916 from Tonbridge on 23 May 1984.

Between High Brooms and Tunbridge Wells was Tunbridge Wells Central Goods Yard and passing here on 1 February 1981 is the first of the class '1301' on the 1138 Tunbridge Wells West to Tonbridge.

The line between Grove Junction, Tunbridge Wells West and Birchden Junction was closed on 6 July 1985 and in its last few weeks I sought out as many new spots to photograph trains as possible. This place overlooking Grove Junction just south of Tunbridge Wells tunnel was very elusive but finally found by a persistent search. I seem to remember my perch was somewhat precarious! Here 1310 is on the 0802 Eridge to Tonbridge on 2 July 1985.

From Grove Junction the line became single and ran past the gardens of some very nice properties before entering a short tunnel under Frant Road, then emerging to pass under Linden Park Road and entering Tunbridge Wells West Station. In this shot taken on 29 May 1985, 1316 is on the 1709 Tonbridge to Eridge. Note the shunting signal arm attached to the up advance starting signal.

On the same day and now facing the other way from the previous shot the signalman in Tunbridge Wells B box is about to hand over the single line token to the driver of 3D 1315 working the 1659 Eridge to Tonbridge. Note how empty the yard is compared to the next shot.

The same location on 14 August 1982 with 3H 1119 stabled on the left and 3D 1312 on the 0934 Eridge to Tonbridge. The magnificent station building survives as a restaurant.

I chose this location just beyond Tunbridge Wells West in order to show the semaphore signals but due to foliage the shot had to be taken in winter. So on 18 January 1981 I was there to photograph 1314 on the 1007 Uckfield to Tonbridge.

Another shot taken on 29 May 1985, this time near to High Rocks, showing 1315 on the 1738 Tonbridge to Eridge service passing the ancient lower quadrant Tunbridge Wells West distant signal. In the far background are the station's home signals.

One of my all-time favourite photo locations from 1961 onwards was Groombridge, and in particular the two footbridges south of the station, both of which are still there today. On 1 July 1985, 1306 is seen leaving Groombridge on the 1738 Tonbridge to Eridge.

Birchden Junction is where the line from Tunbridge Wells joins the main line from Oxted. On 2 July 1985, a few days before closure, 1316 is on the 0811 from Tonbridge to Eridge. The semaphore signal is guarding the junction on the line from Oxted.

The lovely bracket starting signals at Eridge frame 1308 which is shunting to the bay platform ready to form the 0937 to Tonbridge on 1 May 1984. Fortunately the line to Tunbridge Wells has been preserved and is thriving.

Little has changed at Eridge on 26 September 1987 as 3D units 205.101 and 205.007, which had the power car from Hastings unit 1015, arrive with the 1319 from Oxted to Uckfield. The signal box remains but is derelict. After I took this shot I travelled to Oxted and back in 202.001 which was the reformed Hastings unit 1013. My favourite diesel units were refusing to die!

Western Region DMMUs classes 117 and 119

The Pressed Steel class 117 suburban and Gloucester class 119 Cross Country DMMUs were used between Reading and Tonbridge, touching all three Southern Region Divisions. Both had two BUT (AEC/Leyland) 150 bhp diesel motors per power car giving a top speed of 70 mph.

The Western Region three-coach diesel mechanical units (DMMUs) worked the Reading to Tonbridge service for many years and although I never really liked them I took quite a few shots. At Buckland, west of Reigate, class 119 unit L594 is on the 1116 Reading to Tonbridge on 8 April 1983. This journey took 2 hours 25 minutes and even the 'fast' service to Gatwick took 2 hours 15 minutes. Class 119 were otherwise known as Gloucester Cross Country Units.

On 22 October 1983 class 119 L573 is seen entering Penshurst with the 1016 Reading to Tonbridge.

7 September 1985. Class 119 L582 has just left Penshurst and is at Blackhoath Lane on the 0916 Reading to Tonbridge.

A busy scene at Tonbridge West yard on 13 August 1983. Class 117 L404 is nearing its destination with the 1016 from Reading while a 2EPB and 4EPB set is stabled and the yard is full of CCE stock. Semaphore signals still control the yard exit towards Redhill.

CCE = Chief Civil Engineer. During my time on the railway in the 1960s and 70s the CCE was regarded as God. What he said went and he was virtually always right, unlike Network Rail today.

Table

Table 9

Train	0915 Charing Cross to Hastings				
Date	1 May 1984				
Units	1011 + 1019				
Load	12 coaches, 2,000 HP				
Timed by	Author				

	miles	sched	mins	secs	speed
Tunbridge Wells Central	0.00	0.00	00	00	
Grove Jct	0.26		01	01	30
Frant	2.26		04	01	56/60
Wadhurst	4.89		07	03	47*
MP 42	7.60		09	40	72
Stonegate	9.17		11	05	83
MP 46	11.60		12	36	90
Etchingham	13.03		13	36	84
MP 48½	14.10		14	22	82
Robertsbridge	15.19		15	14	78
Mountfield	17.58		17	54	53*
MP 54	19.60		19	20	67
Battle	21.20	24.30	21	12	
	start to stop average exactly 60 mph power on all the way from MP 42 to MP 51 timed from 3rd car back in 1011 * brakes or speed restriction				

CHAPTER SEVEN

DIESEL, ELECTRIC AND ELECTRO DIESEL LOCOMOTIVES

Class 33.0, 33.1 and 33.2 Bo-Bo Diesel Electric Locomotives

Originally numbered D6500-D6597 they were built by the Birmingham Railway Carriage and Wagon Company (BRCW) in 1960-62. Known as 'Cromptons' due to their Crompton Parkinson 305 HP traction motors, they had Sulzer 1,550 BHP engines and a maximum speed of 85 mph. The standard locomotives were renumbered 33.001-33.065 and worked anywhere on the Southern except the Tonbridge to Hastings line. Those later converted for push-pull working for the Bournemouth line electrification scheme were renumbered 33.101-33.119 and in theory only worked on the South Western Division. The locomotives with narrow bodies suitable for the Tonbridge to Hastings line (known as 'Slim Jims') were numbered 33.201-33.212. These weren't confined to the Hastings line and could be found anywhere on the South Eastern Division. The 33s were amongst my favourite locomotives and were given all manner of work, being broadly equivalent to a BR Standard Class 5 on the Southern. They could be very speedy and I once timed one at 94 mph on the Brighton to Plymouth train at Broad Clyst. However I remember them most for their work on the Waterloo to Salisbury semi fast trains 'Table 10 – *See Page 163*' and on the Oxted line peak hour extra trains. A large number are preserved on Heritage Railways and two, D6515 and 33.207, are fitted for main line work and are operational.

To show just how long the class 33s have been active on the Southern this shot was taken at Ramsgate on 11 September 1960 and shows D6516 on the 1730 to Charing Cross. It was taken at the time when Cromptons were only used on summer passenger workings as they were only ETH fitted whereas the Bulleid stock it is hauling was steam heated. In the train heating season they worked multiple with class 24s which were fitted with train heating boilers.

A good place to see class 33s was the CCE depot at Tonbridge West yard. Here on the afternoon of 20 October 1984 are 33.028, 33.202 and 33.209.

The next series of shots is taken on the South Eastern Division, which had no class 33 hauled passenger trains in the period covered by this book (except the *Night Ferry*) but had lots of freight and van trains. Taken from the footbridge east of Paddock Wood on 21 July 1985, 33.042 and 33.060 are unusually double heading the 0827 Paddock Wood to Dover Town ABS Transfesa empty vans, bound for Spain and running about 90 minutes late.

Slightly further east at Queen Street on 16 April 1983, 33.047 is working the 0230 Westbury to Hothfield stone train, which will reverse at Ashford.

Maidstone West on 15 June 1983. 33.056 is on the 1552 Cliffe to Salfords. This was a 'Q' working which ran to either Salfords or Purley, the latter with headcode 6J. It was running 17 minutes early at 1643. I was waiting for the 1632 train home to Paddock Wood which was cancelled as was the next train at 1702 and so I had to catch the 1740 which had EPB 5177. The next day things were even worse so I gave up and caught the No. 6 bus home which was Leyland Atlantean 615 UKM.

Another regular turn for a class 33, this one being a 'Slim Jim', was the 1138 Mountfield to Northfleet stone train. 33.206 is passing Etchingham on 1 May 1984. There appears to be a passenger in the rear cab. Maybe it was the Mountfield shunter.

Wye station facing towards Canterbury was a nice location as the little signalbox could be included in the shot. Here on 10 June 1985 33.001 is heading the 1150 Betteshanger Colliery Sidings to Cricklewood coal train at a time when the Kent Coalfield was still active. Headcode AE should have been shown on this class 6 train, 6M18.

The Folkestone Harbour branch is now defunct but it was still in use on 8 August 1985 when 33.012 is seen climbing the 1-in-36 with the 1515 VSOE Pullman to London Victoria. On the rear of the train is 73.134 which would take the train on from Folkestone East sidings after reversal there. 33.012 would remain at Folkestone.

As referred to earlier, the *Night Ferry* was the only regular class 33 passenger working on the South Eastern division. On 30 October 1980, during its last week of operation, 33.043 is passing Tonbridge on the up train, which is a mere shadow of its former self. The consist is two Fourgon vans, six Wagon Lits sleeping cars and a MK1 brake 1st. The last down train on 31 October was also hauled by 33.043 and I saw this passing Paddock Wood at 10.16 pm. The last up train on 1 November was a class 73. More images of the *Night Ferry* are in the sections on class 71s and 73s.

Class 33s worked the Lydd stone trains and I got a few photos of these workings on the interesting but often bleak Romney Marsh. Brookland station lost its passenger service in March 1967 but the station building is still intact on 6 April 1976 as 33.204 passes with a stone train from Lydd.

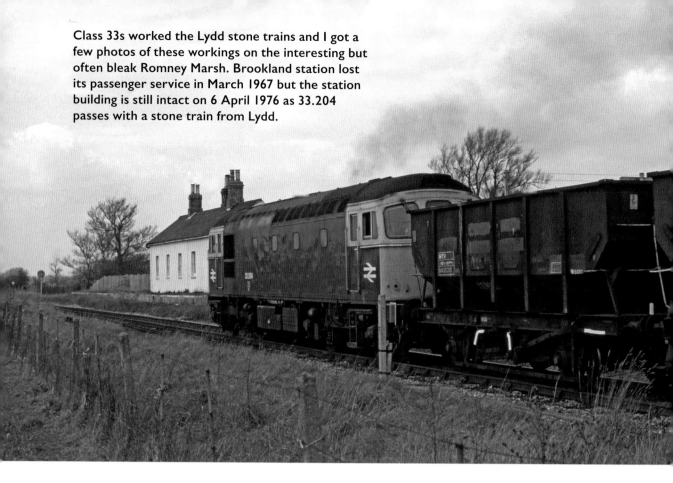

In deep mid-winter on 12 January 1987 33.044 is passing Paddock Wood at 1008 running light engine towards Tonbridge. The mercury stands at minus 7 centigrade and the up through line is blocked due to frozen points. But trains are running; see the section on severe winters.

West of Tonbridge and nearly into Central Division territory at Edenbridge on a very cold and frosty 19 March 1985, 33.059 is on 7R68, the 0911 Tonbridge to Redhill CCE ballast train. Headcode 8J should be showing.

On the Central Division class 33s had a number of diagrams on peak hour trains from Uckfield and East Grinstead to London Bridge. I spent a lot of time photographing and travelling on these and one of my favourite locations was Chellows Lane between Lingfield and Hurst Green. Here on the beautiful morning of 29 May 1985 33.054 is on the 0826 East Grinstead to London Bridge.

In very different conditions on a very cold 19 March 1985, 33.025 is seen on the same train leaving Lingfield. The stock for this train worked down on the 0726 from East Croydon. 33025 was named *Sultan* between 8 August 1981 and 1 May 1988 and then again between 31 January 1989 and 28 February 1997.

Nearly two years earlier, on 21 April 1983, 33.211 is on the same train passing Selsdon. The signalman's bike is parked on the platform used by trains from Elmers End to Sanderstead and I had arrived in 2 EPB 5723 on the 0832 from Sanderstead. The line was closed soon after my visit on 13 May 1983.

On the same day, during which I spent time at a number of locations photographing SR emus, I found myself at London Bridge to photograph the evening peak services. 33.056 *The Burma Star* was on the 1720 to Uckfield and 33.014 on the 1734 to East Grinstead. I caught the latter to Oxted and it lost time due to various checks but sustained 36 mph on the 1-in-100 to Riddlesdown with its eight-coach 280 ton load.

Loco haulage on the 1720 from London Bridge to Uckfield ceased with the timetable change in May 1984. Push-Pull fitted 33.107 worked the last train on 11 May 1984 and it is seen here passing the site of Redgate Mill Junction with a suitable headboard and many enthusiasts on board.

The return working at 1910 from Uckfield to East Croydon on the same evening is seen descending the 1-in-100 to Hever from the 1,060 yard long tunnel. This was another favourite spot in the days of steam, for which I had a lineside pass in 1963.

On the South Western Division main line the 33s worked the Waterloo to Salisbury semi fast trains. Most of these were 33.1s working push pull with a TC unit, but some were comprised of loco hauled MK 1 and/or MK 2 stock. Here 33.007 is on the six-coach 1410 Waterloo to Salisbury on the down slow line at Old Basing on 19 April 1984.

33.051 is at Salisbury with the same 1410 from Waterloo on a sunny 22 October 1986. I had arrived there behind 33.002 on the 1410 from Portsmouth which on five coaches ran early throughout. The next image shows one of these cross country trains.

Just west of Salisbury and where the lines from Exeter and Westbury are combined was a lovely photo location at Bemerton where the spire of Salisbury cathedral could be included in the shot. The white house on the right is still there but the view of the cathedral is now obscured by growth in lineside trees and bushes which is so common now. This view was taken on 10 March 1988 and shows 33.026 on the 1210 Portsmouth to Cardiff.

On the same day 33.040 and 33.049 are on the heavy 0634 Three Bridges to Meldon Quarry CCE empty ballast train. They are passing a class 56 on a Westbury stone train.

On 25 April 1988 the same train is passing Stockton between Wilton Junction and Warminster. It would reverse at Westbury and again at Exeter.

Also between Warminster and Wilton Junction, this time at Wylye on 25 April 1988, 33.033 is on the 0950 Swansea to Portsmouth. I made three visits to this area in the spring of 1988 to capture the class 33s at work before they were superseded on the Portsmouth trains by Sprinters. These trains ran about every two hours and were usually formed of five MK1 coaches. The Sprinters run hourly but are only three coaches and often have standing passengers at peak times.

Class 47 Diesel Locomotives

A total of 512 of these Type 4 locomotives were built in the 1960s, with many variations on the basic theme which was a 2,750 BHP (later de-rated to 2580 BHP) Co-Co Brush engined locomotive intended primarily for express passenger work. There were a number of sub classes but as these locos were employed mainly on Inter Regional trains to Bournemouth, Portsmouth, Brighton and Dover and not native to the Southern, I will not explore all the detail here. However any true Southern enthusiast cannot forget and forgive that they were substituted for steam locomotives on the latter days of the *Bournemouth Belle*, including the very last day this service ran. They were originally numbered in the D1500-D1999 and D1100-D1111 series, renumbered to the series 47.001-47.981. A large number are still in service on Heritage lines and on the main line. They had a rated top speed of 95 mph though I timed them at over 100 mph on the Western and London Midland Regions as well as an extraordinary run on the South Eastern main line where 47.613 reached 107 mph. Table 11 – *See Page 164.*

In the 1980s class 47s were quite widely used throughout the Southern, mainly on Inter Regional trains and also on some freight hauls. They certainly provided welcome variety from the standard diet of multiple units on the South Eastern Division, especially as some drivers used their full 95 mph capability (see page 164). On 4 October 1986, a class 47, number not recorded, is near Paddock Wood travelling at close to 100 mph with the 1045 Dover Western Docks to Liverpool Lime Street.

On 16 August 1987, 47.537 is seen passing Paddock Wood with the 1100 Victoria to Folkestone Harbour VSOE Pullman. This train was usually worked by class 73 EDLs until 1986. Ten minutes before the VSOE, 47.464 in green livery had passed at high speed on the 1033 Kensington Olympia to Dover Western Docks. A 4 CEP waits in the platform with the late running 1100 Charing Cross to Ashford stopping service which had been held for both class 47 hauled trains.

Also near Paddock Wood and seen from the same footbridge, green liveried 47.500 *Great Western* is resplendent on the 1045 Dover Western Docks to Liverpool Lime Street on Christmas Eve 1986. The track on the right was the start of the branch line to Hawkhurst.

On 29 August 1987, 47.508 is entering Dover Western Docks station with a train from Liverpool Lime Street.

On 31 August 1987, 47.618 is at Dover Western Docks station with the 0740 from Manchester Piccadilly. It would return on the 1354 via Chatham which I caught as far as Canterbury East. The 47 did well on nine coaches with a minimum speed of 62 at Shepherdswell and 89 mph after Adisham.

Over on the South Western Division at Dunbridge on the line from Salisbury to Romsey, 47.256 is on the 0803 Whateley to Totton stone train on 10 March 1988.

On 19 April 1984, 47.363 is working oil tanks on the down slow line at Old Basing.

Finally in this section on the class 47s, on 20 October 1986, 47.594 pauses at Basingstoke with the 1438 Poole to Manchester Piccadilly. The loco is clean but the MK 2 stock less so. I had been on this train from Poole and with ten coaches for about 335 tons it had kept time without any great effort. When a batch of 47s came to the Southern to help out steam in the autumn of 1966 they were shunned by the steam fraternity!

Class 50 Diesel Locomotives

Fifty of these powerful Co-Co diesel electric locomotives were built by English Electric at the Vulcan Foundry and were initially leased to British Rail. They had English Electric 16 CSVT diesel engines powering EE538 400 HP traction motors and were rated at 2,700 BHP with a top speed of 100 mph. Initially numbered D400-D449 they became 50.001-50.050. As far as the Southern is concerned they worked the Exeter services for some years and proved to be very fast in service reaching their top speed even on sections of route limited to 85 mph. **Table 12** – *See Page 165*. They were, however, unreliable and non-standard and were withdrawn in the 1990s. Remarkably for a relatively small class of locomotive, eighteen have been preserved.

Although not indigenous to the Southern, the class 50s worked the Waterloo to Exeter service from 1983 until 1992 and so qualify for inclusion in this book. They were very powerful and speedy machines but unreliable. On 18 February 1983, 50.037 is seen approaching Clapham Junction with the 1110 Waterloo to Exeter.

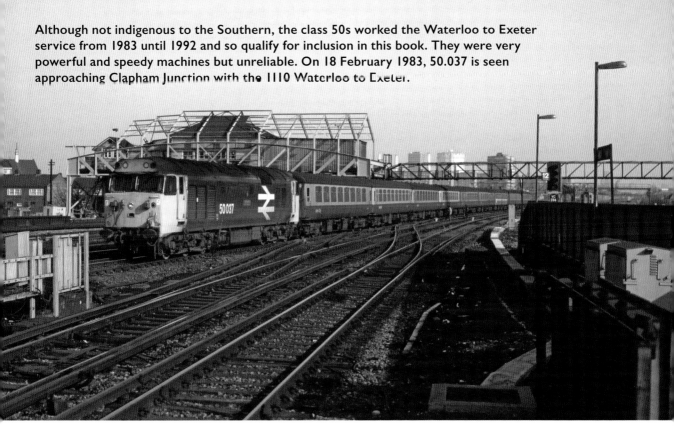

Also at Clapham Junction, this time on 24 October 1983, 50.001 is on the 1510 Waterloo to Exeter.

On 3 November 1985, 50.041 is at Old Basing on the 1110 Waterloo to Exeter.

Salisbury on 28 February 1986. 50.035 has arrived on the 1110 from Waterloo. I had travelled on this train from Woking and the 50 had gained time throughout, reaching 94 mph after Hook and 93 mph down Porton bank on jointed track.

In full NSE colours 50.034 is seen leaving Salisbury on 10 March 1988 with the 1203 Portsmouth Harbour to Paignton. This train was the successor to the Brighton to Plymouth train.

Class 50s were popular for Railtours but it was very unusual to see one on the South Eastern Division. On 15 March 1986 50.025 worked an 0755 Paddington to Ashford and is seen near Strawberry Hill tunnel south of Tunbridge Wells.

Class 71 Bo-Bo Electric Locomotives

Originally numbered E5000-E5023, these powerful, economical and reliable Bo-Bo electric locos were built at Doncaster in 1958 for the Kent Coast Lines. They had four EE532 traction motors giving 2,552 HP with a top speed of 90 mph. They were used on freight, van trains and the prestigious *Golden Arrow*, and also worked the heavy *Night Ferry*.

Unfortunately the goods traffic for which they were built quickly disappeared and being straight electrics their use was limited. In 1967 ten were rebuilt as Class 74 electro diesels, which were not a success as, unlike their donor locomotives, they were not reliable. Remaining locos were renumbered 71.001-71.014. All but E5001, which is preserved as part of the National Collection, were withdrawn by 1977 due to having no work.

In August 1961, two months after the end of steam, E5015 is passing Chelsfield with the down *Golden Arrow*, with full regalia.

Just ten years later, on 25 July 1971, E5104 is seen at Smeeth on the up *Golden Arrow* but with no headboard or flags. At that time it was quite unusual for the train to be identified other than by the 46 headcode and of course the Pullmans.

The last down *Golden Arrow* on 30 September 1972 did carry headboard and flags and is seen here at Sevington, east of Ashford, with E5013 in charge. So the long period when I saw this train, during which it was hauled by Britannia class pacifics *William Shakespeare* and *Iron Duke* plus Bulleid Merchant Navy class pacifics and last of all in the steam era, Bulleid light pacific 34100 *Appledore*, comes to an end.

By 9 February 1976 when this shot was taken, the class had been renumbered into the 71 series. 71.009 has just passed Paddock Wood on a Dover to Bricklayers Arms mixed van train.

At the same location a few weeks later on 4 March 1976, but earlier in the day, 71.014 is heading the up *Night Ferry*, 0720 Dover Marine to Victoria. The consist was normal for that time, comprising two Fourgon vans, seven Wagon Lits Sleepers and a MK1 brake 1st. When I first started to photograph this train in 1960 it could load up to fifteen vehicles, or about 800 tons.

Journey's end for the *Night Ferry* at Victoria on 7 October 1971. It is arriving at Platform 2, which is still used today for most loco-hauled charter trains. The 75 headcode indicates that it had operated via Chatham and the Catford Loop line. Another class 71 waits at the buffer stops on Platform 1 to take the stock out.

Class 73.0 and Class 73.1 Bo-Bo Electro Diesel Locomotives

Originally numbered E6001-6006, the first batch (SR designation JA), later numbered 73.001-73.006, were built at Eastleigh in 1962 and were fitted with English Electric 4SRKT 600 BHP diesel engines and four EE 542A 400 HP traction motors. These had a top speed of 80 mph. A later batch, E6007-6049 (73.101-73.142) (SR designation JB), were built by Vulcan Foundry between 1965 and 1967 and had EE 546 traction motors, giving a higher tractive effort and with a maximum speed of 90

mph. They could work with class 33/1 diesels and compatible multiple units which they did for a time on the Western Division. **Table 13** – *See Page 166*. These versatile locomotives worked on all three divisions. In 1988 a twelve strong sub-class – 73/2 – was formed from 73/1s to create a dedicated fleet of electro diesels for Gatwick Express. In 1995 two 73/0s were transferred to Merseyrail, redesignated 73/90, for Sandite duties. Thirteen have been rebuilt as Class 73.95 and 73.96 for further work, much of which can be away from the Southern. Other class 73s have been preserved and run on heritage railways.

Most of my shots of the Electro Diesels were taken on the South Eastern Division but here is one of 73.001 passing under Clapham Junction, signal box A on 24 October 1983 with ballast wagons from the Western Region. This is a WR to Chessington Branch, Tolworth working.

On the Central Division the EDLs worked Gatwick Express trains from 1984 until 2005. Here, 73.127 in BR 'Mainline' colours and 73.138 are at Gatwick on 6 August 1985.

73127 is, as described at the time, in 'Mainline' (later known as Intercity Executive) colours, 73138 is in large logo blue. There were not ever many EDLs in NSE livery and they wore the well-known red 'white' blue & grey 'toothpaste' stripes. The 1984 Gatwick Express service started out as part of the Brighton main line modernization project as a London & SE sector project but using Intercity colours from its inception, presumably for perception reasons. In May 1985 it was controversially transferred to the Intercity Sector. Presumably because it was already a good little earner.

Also on 6 August 1985, 73.141 is on a CCE track train at Redhill while another class 73 lurks in the background. I then travelled to Gatwick on the 1140 train with CIG 7396 and 7398.

The class 73s were very versatile and could be called on to perform almost any duty. At Snodland on 25 August 1983, 73.114 is piloting 33.057 on 1405 Hoo Junction to Salfords oil tank train. This train was booked for class 33 haulage so maybe the Class 73 was taken to save a train path.

A regular EDL working in the mid-1980s was the 0955 Ramsgate to London Bridge empty parcels and coaching stock service. This train returned the stock of the various overnight mail trains back to London and was much photographed by myself. On a bright and sunny 3 November 1984, 73.102 is passing Paddock Wood at 75 mph. This shot was taken with my trusty Pentax KX 35 mm camera on Kodachrome 25 asa film at 1/500 shutter speed with the aperture at F2.8, showing the quality that could be obtained in those far off pre-digital days.

The same train in Folkestone Warren on 8 August 1985. It is being hauled by the same loco, 73.102. On 30 April 1985 it was transmogrified into BR 'Mainline' colours and named *Airtour Suisse*. It is carrying the incorrect headcode 55, as C1 'as shown in the previous shot' is correct for this working.

The last *Night Ferry* from Paris ran on 31 October 1980 and so ran up from Dover for the last time on Saturday, 1 November 1980. Unusually it was headed by a class 73 instead of a class 33, and 73.142 *Broadlands* is seen passing Paddock Wood pre-dawn at 0646. Even my Pentax couldn't produce a decent colour shot and so this was taken by my Bronica ETR-C using Kodak Tri X 400 asa film.

Remaining shots of the class 73s are all taken of the class hauling the VSOE Pullman which ran from 25 May 1982 between London Victoria and Folkestone Harbour where passengers were transferred to steamer for the crossing to Calais and onwards by VSOE European stock to Paris and Venice. In its first year of operation, 73.120 is seen east of Paddock Wood on the down train on 25 July 1982.

On 3 July 1983, 73.122 is on the down train, 1144 from Victoria, in Bickley cutting.

The last rays of the setting sun pick out 73.121 on the up train, 1540 Folkestone Harbour to Victoria at Charing Heath, having been diverted from the main line via Tonbridge by Engineering work. The date is 23 October 1983. This is one of my favourite pictures of the many I took of this train. Pentax KX 1/125 second at F2 on Kodachrome 25 asa film.

At Whetsted, just west of Paddock Wood on the beautiful spring day of 29 April 1984, 73.101 *Brighton Evening Argus* is on the up VSOE Pullman. The whole train is absolutely immaculate in the sun. 73101 gained this name in December 1980 as part of the celebrations of the 100th anniversary of the eponymous local newspaper. In 1992 it was repainted into Pullman umber and cream and temporarily renamed *The Royal Alex*, except that the original name was not reinstated.

73.142 *Broadlands* was a frequent performer on the VSOE and is seen here passing Hollingbourne at about 80 mph on the retimed and diverted 1605 Folkestone Harbour to Victoria, but without the headboard and looking decidedly travel-stained. The date is 20 April 1986.

Folkestone Harbour on 8 August 1985. 73.134 is bringing the 1415 empty stock slowly down from Folkestone East to form the 1540 working to Victoria. On the back is 33.012 which will pull the train back up to the east sidings before it reverses and 73.134 takes it on to London. The branch is closed but mothballed so who knows what the future holds?

At Folkestone Harbour passengers from the train in the previous shot would have transfered to a ferry for Calais, but not this one as this is the *Caesarea* arriving on the 1005 from Calais on 24 September 1980 during it's last week in service. It was the last steam turbine and classic cross channel ferry. Built in Cowes in 1960 it worked out of Weymouth to the Channel Islands until 1975 before being transferred to the short sea crossings. After withdrawal by Sealink it spent time in the far east before being broken up in 1986. I loved the handsome steam turbine ships, my favourite being *Invicta* (Denny of Dumbarton 1940) which normally worked the *Golden Arrow* service, and also *St Patrick* which, when it was working the Folkestone to Boulogne service in 1971, had a permanent list which showed when sitting a pint of beer on the bar!

Tables

Table 10

CLASS 33 BASINGSTOKE TO WOKING

Date	20 October 1986
Train	1315 Salisbury to Waterloo
Engine	Class 33/1 Bo-Bo 33.136
Load	8 coaches and 2 vans, 334 tons tare, 345 tons gross
Recorder	Author

	miles	sched	mins	secs	speed	
Basingstoke	0.00	0.00	00	00		1 late
MP 46	1.75		02	54	57	
Newnham Siding (Site)	4.10		04	59	70½	
Hook	5.59		06	16	73	
MP 41	6.75		07	14	75	
Winchfield	7.92		08	10	78	
MP 38	9.75		09	31	82½	
Fleet	11.27		10	37	82	
MP 35	12.75		11	43	84	
Farnborough	14.55		13	01	82	
Sturt Lane	15.60		13	46	81	
MP 31	16.75		14	41	78	
Pirbright Junction	18.26		15	42	82	
Brookwood	19.76		16	53	83	
MP 27	20.75		17	37	80	
Woking Junction	23.00		20	59	22*	tsr
Woking	23.46	22.00	21	54		1 late
	net time 20½ minutes start to stop average 64.27 mph					

Table 11

CLASS 47- ASHFORD TO TONBRIDGE

Train	1754 Dover Western Docks to Manchester Piccadilly		
Date	31 August 1987		
Loco	47.613		
Load	7 coaches plus 1 van, 269½ tons tare, 280 tons gross		
Timed by	Author		
Weather	Sunny and hot, slight SE breeze		

	miles	mins	secs	speed
Ashford	0.00	00	00	
Chart Siding (site)	2.11	03	05	66
Pluckley	5.67	05	43	92
MP 49	7.11	06	37	94
MP 46	10.11	08	28	104
Headcorn	10.86	08	55	105
MP 43	13.11	10	11	107
Staplehurst	14.25	10	51	103
Marden	16.72	12	16	101
MP 38	18.11	13	05	102
MP 36	20.11	14	19	97/95
Paddock Wood	21.29	15	03	98
MP 33	23.11	16	11	96
MP 31	25.11	17	32	78*
		sigs		14*
Tonbridge	26.59	20	34	
	Average MP46-MP38	103.97 mph		
	Pluckley-Paddock Wood	100.45 mph		
	Start to stop average	77.57 mph		
	net time 19½ minutes			

Table 12

CLASS 50-BASINGSTOKE TO SALISBURY

Date	22 October 1986
Train	0910 Waterloo to Exeter
Loco	50.026
Load	8 coaches, 256½ tons tare, 275 tons gross
Timed by	Author
Weather	Rain

	miles	sched	mins	secs	speed	
Basingstoke	0.00	0.00	00	00		1 min late
Worting Jct	2.55	4.00	03	26	62	
MP 51	3.35		04	07	67	
Oakley	4.63		05	13	80	
MP 53½	5.80		06	08	82	
Overton	7.80		07	32	93	
Whitchurch	11.35		09	49	98	
Hurstbourne	13.39		11	00	102	
MP 62½	14.85		11	53	90	eased
Andover	18.60	17.30	15	21		
	0.00	0.00	00	00		right time
Red Post Jct	1.30		02	13	52½	
MP 68¾	2.50		03	21	70	
MP 71	4.75		05	11	75½	
Grateley	6.35		06	29	74	
Allington Box	9.25		08	42	88	
Porton	11.90		10	26	100	
MP 81	14.75		12	13	96	brakes
MP 82¼	16.00		sigs stop		0*	
Tunnel Junction	16.21	15.30	17	22	36/2*	sigs
Salisbury	17.31	17.30	20	27		
	net time Andover to Salisbury 15¼ minutes					

Table 13

CLASS 73s -BASINGSTOKE TO WOKING

Date	27 April 1988	1 October 1988
Train	1400 Bournemouth to Waterloo	1046 Bournemouth to Waterloo
Engine	Class 73 Bo-Bo 73.135	Class 73 Bo-Bos 73.132 and 73.130
Load	5TCB 2807+4TC 8016, 298 tons tare, 320 tons gross	5TCB 2804+4TC 8036
Timed by	Author	Author

	miles	sched	mins	secs	speed		sched	mins	secs	speed	
Basingstoke	0.00	0.00	00	00		3 late		00	00		
MP 46	1.75		03	11	66½			02	45	70½	
Newnham Siding (Site)	4.10		05	05	75			04	26	84	
Hook	5.59		06	13	80			05	26	88	
MP 41	6.75		07	08	82			06	16	92	
Winchfield	7.92		08	00	83½			07	00	93	
MP 38	9.75		09	17	86½			08	11	95	
Fleet	11.27		10	19	87			09	06	96	
MP 35	12.75		11	21	86			10	03	97	
Farnborough	14.55		12	34	85			11	10	92	
Sturt Lane	15.60		13	19	84			11	52	93	
MP 31	16.75		14	10	82½			12	39	90	
Pirbright Junction	18.26		15	08	88			13	33	95	
Brookwood	19.76		16	11	91			14	31	98	
MP 27	20.75		16	50	92			15	09	90/44*	sigs
Woking Junction	23.00		18	34	55*	brakes		17	34	60	
Woking	23.46	19.30	19	17		3 late		17	57	63	pass
	start to stop average 73.0 mph						MP41-MP27=94.56 mph				

CHAPTER EIGHT

DEPARTMENTAL STOCK

These comprised Stores and De-Icing units, converted from withdrawn emus. The Stores units worked to regular timetables though I simply photographed them when they appeared, not knowing the times that one would be due.

Stores unit 022 at Orpington on 30 September 1982. This was converted from 2 HAL units 2613 and 2669. Stores unit 023 was also converted from 2 HAL units, this one from 2624 and 2642. 022 was replaced by 019 from January 1983; see next page.

Stores unit 024, seen here passing Paddock Wood on the 1139 Stewarts Lane to Chart Leacon on 3 November 1984, was converted from 4 SUB 4378. It's in rather dull Olive Green colours.

M&EE Stores unit 019, converted from 2 HAP 5629, is at Hastings on 29 August 1987. The up starting semaphore signals are in the process of being converted to colour lights. M&EE = Mechanical and Electrical Engineer.

De-Icing unit 005 at Clapham Junction on 24 October 1983. The headcode indicates that it's going to Norwood Junction. It was converted from 4 SUB unit 4121.

Inspection Car TDS 70155 being propelled on the up through line at Ashford by 33.210 on 14 September 1976. It was used mainly for driver training and route learning and was converted from Maunsell Hastings line CK S5600S in 1962, which was built in 1931.

CHAPTER NINE
SEVERE WINTERS

This section contains images of the trains on the South Eastern Division during the severe spells of winter weather in 1985 and 1987. Unlike the fragmented and often unreliable railway today the first priority then was to keep trains running whatever the conditions and it would do some of our railway managers a lot of good to look through this section and learn what can be done in some quite appalling conditions. Today services are unbelievably withdrawn or truncated with the mere threat of snow, with more thought of who might pay if things go wrong or damage to the multiple units when snow falls than providing a service to the people that matter. The culture that existed in the 1970s and 80s simply doesn't exist now. The railway then certainly wasn't perfect and the modern railway has made some big strides forward, but it could be so much better if organised differently and with clear direction from the top.

Of the many spells of severe winter weather which affected the South Eastern Division in the period covered by this book, the worst were in 1985 and 1987. Unlike today, trains kept running of course, and here at Paddock Wood on 6 January 1985, 4 CEP 1572 is heading the 0922 Ashford to Charing Cross semi fast service while 73.109 waits in the down slow platform with the 0808 parcels from Maidstone West to Tonbridge.

On 8 January more snow had fallen overnight and temperature locally fell to -14°C. Running on time, 4 VEP 7886 is leading the 0647 Ramsgate to Cannon Street at Paddock Wood. I was waiting for my 0802 train to Maidstone West, which was cancelled, but the 0821 ran five minutes late with 4 VEP 7778. My train home that evening was the 1650 which ran on time with 4 CEP 1583.

The severe spell continued and on 14 January 1985 it snowed all day so by the morning of the 15th there was about six inches lying on the ground with the temperature at -2°C. My journey to and from Maidstone was untroubled on the 14th but the extreme conditions on the 15th resulted in some delays. I caught the 0659 from Paddock Wood which ran 65 minutes late with 4 CEP 1587 and, as more snow was falling during the day, decided to make my way home early. This shot shows an unidentified 4 VEP at Maidstone West on the 1421 Paddock Wood to Strood service, unbelievably on time. There isn't the slightest chance of any train services of today running in such conditions, let alone those on the third rail system.

My train, the 1421 from Strood, appeared about five minutes late with 4 CEP 1542 and with the snow lying now at twelve inches deep and above rail level in many places; even the sturdy old CEP had difficulty starting away from stops. With the mercury at -3°C it's a wonder anything moved at all. Just look at the snow and ice on the bogies of the VEP.

Journey's end at Paddock Wood with 1542, though the crew are preparing to take the train back to Strood at 1521. The 1425 Charing Cross to Ramsgate is signaled on the down slow platform. I just plodded home in the deep snow. The thaw set in on 18 January after fourteen days of lying snow.

January 1987 saw another spell of severe weather and conditions were worse than in 1985 so trains services suffered more. For instance there was no service on the Maidstone West branch from Paddock Wood for most of the week beginning 12 January, though trains still ran on the main line via Paddock Wood. In this shot taken on Sunday, 11 January a 4CEP is working the 0910 Charing Cross to Ashford stopping service.

This was followed at 1034 by an up Ashford stopping train.

As no more snow was falling I decided to drive to Bearsted on the Maidstone East to Ashford line where the snow promptly started to fall again, almost obliterating the 4 CEP on the 1407 Ashford to Victoria stopping service.

Conditions got gradually worse and I had just decided to abandon my session when at 1505 an 8 CEP formation came into view through the blizzard on what I think was the diverted 1243 Ramsgate to Charing Cross train running about 45 minutes late. These were the worst conditions that I ever photographed trains in, except maybe on the Reine to Emden line in Germany in January 1972. At Bearsted the temperature had fallen to -6°C but my drive home through deep snow wasn't as bad as I expected as nobody else was stupid enough to be out.

The next day, 12 January, was sunny but very cold with a maximum temperature of -7°C locally. 4 CEP 1550 is leading an 8 CEP formation on the 0827 Margate to Charing Cross stopping train. Note the up fast line not in use.

Remaining shots were taken on 13 January when it snowed on and off all day. The main-line timetable had been abandoned due to the severity of conditions and now damage being done to the electrical gear on the emus. This produced some interesting formations in an effort to try to maintain a service. Here Tadpole 206.101 is on a down train just east of Paddock Wood at 1350 hours.

Even more amazing, at 1430, 47.131
appeared hauling an 8 CEP formation which
included 1526. Note both fast lines out
of use due to points failures despite the
obvious efforts to keep them operational.

On the bitterly cold day of 13 January 1987 we see 33.042 sandwiched between two
snow ploughs approaching Paddock Wood from the east, presumably returning from
duties elsewhere in Kent where twenty-five inches of snow had fallen in places.

EPILOGUE

Finally, and not wanting to finish on a negative note, I have included shots of my two favourite classes from the Southern after the end of steam. Here, close to my home of twenty-five years, is CEP 1574 passing Paddock Wood on a lovely autumn evening, 7 September 1985. It's on the 1529 Ramsgate to Charing Cross service.

If I had to choose my all-time favourites, it would be the Hastings diesels. So, last of all, 6S units 1007 and 1006 are seen here climbing to Polhill tunnel past the site of the long-closed signal box, working the last Hastings diesel-operated 0714 Hastings to Charing Cross on 25 April 1986.

ACKNOWLEDGEMENTS

With grateful thanks to Colin Duff for checking the draft of this book and for adding to and correcting the text. His detailed knowledge of all things Southern far exceeds mine. Thanks also to the Southern Electric Group, of which I have been a member for many years. Their house magazine *Live Rail* is an invaluable source of reference. Any errors in the text are mine and mine alone.

BIBLIOGRAPHY

Southern Region Multiple Unit Trains – G.D. Beecroft, Southern Electric Group

Southern Region Two-Character Headcodes – G.D. Beecroft and B.W. Rayner, (various years) Southern Electric Group

Southern Electric Group-House magazine *Live Rail* and its website, southernelectric.org.uk

Southern Railway E-Group website, semgonline.com

The 4 Sub Story - Bryan Rayner & David Brown, Southern Electric Group

British Multiple Units, Volume 2, EPBs, Haps, Saps and Cap – Ashley Butlin, Coorlea Publishing

British Multiple Units, Volume 4, Classes 410-490 & 508 – Ashley Butlin, Coorlea Publishing

Southern Electric Multiple-Units 1898-1948 - Colin J. Marsden, Ian Allan

Southern Electric Multiple-Units 1948-1983 - Colin J. Marsden, Ian Allan

British Railways Locomotives and other motive power, Combined Volume 1975 - Alan Williams and David Percival, Ian Allan

Modern Locomotives Illustrated, No.214, Southern Design Electric Multiple Units -edited by Colin J. Marsden, Key Publishing

Modern Locomotives Illustrated, No.220, BR Southern Region Electric Multiple Units - edited by Colin J. Marsden, Key Publishing

Modern Locomotives Illustrated, No.198, The Electro-Diesels Classes 73 and 74 - edited by Colin J. Marsden, Key Publishing

Modern Locomotives Illustrated, No.215, DC Electric Locos - edited by Colin J. Marsden, Key Publishing

Encyclopaedia of Modern Traction Names - Colin J. Marsden & Darren Ford, Channel AV Publishing